I'LL BAKE!

I'LL BAKE!

Something delicious for every occasion

Liberty
Mendez

PAVILION

INTRODUCTION

There's always an occasion for a bake. Whether you invite your friends around last minute and need a speedy dessert to devour while gossiping about 'that person' you shouldn't be talking to, or you need a snack to shovel into your face while binge-watching a reality show on a dark evening, or you want to save some money and make an afternoon tea at home for the in-laws – baking is always the answer.

Do you want to be the legend who enters the party clutching a cake box, that everyone's excited to see? The person who brings the cake makes the party. It's a fact, I've decided. Nothing will beat the elation that the lucky recipient has on their face when they see the sweet masterpiece you've created, even if it has been knocked ever so slightly on the journey there. The fact that you've poured your heart into making something to bring that person delight, will never go amiss. When everyone's discussing what they'll bring to a dinner party or weekend away, be the one who shouts, 'I'll Bake!'. If you're already the designated dessert person, I hope that this book helps give you ideas on how to take the celebration to the next level.

Whether it's clutching a carrot cake dressed as Britney Spears on a train to a 90s party, running through the rain to a barn in the middle of a forest with an intricate wedding cake, icing a Mr Blobby-inspired cake at 2am or losing the feeling in my arms from an hour on the London tube's rush hour at 30°C holding a melting cheesecake for a friend's birthday – it's been my mission to be the one that bakes… every time. Rain or shine, there WILL be dessert.

There's a running joke between me and most of my friends – that the only reason I have secured and maintained our friendship is because I constantly provide them with baked goods. Which is only *partially* true. Cake makes people happy. So it's no surprise that baking cakes has become my people-pleasing security blanket, a sure-fire way of providing joy, and the main reason I became a pastry chef. (That, and I *really* enjoy being sworn at, locked in freezers and waking up at 4am. Not.)

Baking doesn't have to be scary, not when you're doing it from the comfort of your own home and for the purpose of bringing joy. I've been a chef for over a decade, and a recipe developer for five years, and have learnt over those years how to make a failproof recipe – providing you follow the recipes (if you want to use gram flour instead of plain flour or jam instead of caster sugar, you're on your own), these will be winners in your household.

My goal was to take the fear out of baking and write recipes at different skill levels, so you can really progress while using this book. You could start off making a loaf cake to bring to a party, or coconut mousse if you're hosting a dinner party, and in no time you'll be whipping up a baked cheesecake for your best friend's cousin's flatmate!

While I was writing and testing this book, I was living in a chaotic and fabulous household with flatmates who were vegan and gluten free – so I was hyper-aware of allergens and wanted there to be a selection of recipes for friends and family who may have dietary requirements. (And also, it benefitted me, because they actually got to try the goods from recipe testing, too. Recipe tasters = friends for life.) I wanted those recipes to be universal, too – even if you don't have any restrictions, they're just as delicious. There's a dietary index at the back of the book indicating which recipes are gluten-free, vegan and dairy-free, which I hope will help! I know that not everyone has a cupboard dedicated to cake tins (a girl can dream), so I've also included a useful list/index at the back detailing the tin/dish sizes, etc, that were used in the book, so if you only have a 900g/2lb loaf tin or an 18cm/7in round cake tin, you know which recipes you can whip up!

TUNES
I can't tell you how excited I am for this part of I'll Bake! As well as baking, music has been an important part of my life (let's not mention the rock band I drummed in at high school). The music you listen to during the occasions that you bake for is almost just as important as the bakes as it sets the atmosphere. I've included QR codes on each chapter that let you access six specially curated Spotify playlists (more information on how to scan can be found here: https://support.spotify.com/us/article/share-from-spotify/). This is the music I always have playing, and it covers everything from dancing around the kitchen while baking to the perfect songs I have playing in the background when enjoying a chilled dinner, and even tunes to get people dancing after you've brought out the cake at a party. I'm thrilled that many of my friends are talented up-and-coming musicians, so I hope you discover their new bangers while listening to the playlists and support the artists – please let me know which ones are your favourites! Thank you for the suggestions some of you sent to me on Instagram, too.

I read something recently (okay, saw it on Instagram) from Sam Schedler. To paraphrase, he said that you're not going to die without a slice of cake, but that's the very reason that we bake. It's to invest time into excess that will bring a little moment of happiness to someone you care about. Which I feel is the sentiment behind this book and why we all bake.

Whenever there's an instance when you could bake, I hope you take it and use the recipes in the book to spread a bit of joy and comfort.

CHEF'S NOTES

A few specifics which will help you understand the technicalities in the recipes.

British and American terms

The recipes in this book use British terms. I have provided imperial and US cup measurements, where appropriate, and some common American terminology can be found on page 179.

Eggs

When I'm baking with eggs, I keep them at room temperature. This is important when you're making a sponge mixture, as keeping all the ingredients at the same temperature stops the mixture from splitting.

I know how expensive it can be to buy large eggs and the size tends to change anyway between brands, so I've made it my mission to create recipes that can still work with whatever size eggs you use, which is why there isn't always a size given. For the recipes where I have given egg sizes, this is because it is specific to the consistency of a recipe (for example, something like cookie dough needs the right amount of liquid so you can roll it easily).

Chocolate

I don't want you to feel pressured to buy very expensive dark chocolate, especially for baking, so any dark chocolate will work, however, I tend to use 70% dark chocolate as it's rich without being too bitter. If you're baking for someone who is vegan or dairy free, make sure the dark chocolate is vegan.

Milk

In certain recipes, like in the Espresso Custard Tart (page 106) and a few others, it's important that you use full-fat milk due to the fat content. However, for all the other recipes that specify using milk, you can either use semi-skimmed or full-fat milk, or, if it's specified in the recipe, a vegan alternative. Although you technically can use any dairy-free milk with vegan cooking, I tend to use soy milk as it's got a higher protein content, so for recipes that need a lot of structure, like a sponge, it's the best dairy-free alternative.

Dairy-free, gluten-free and vegan recipes

I've tried to make these recipes as accessible as possible in terms of allergens. As well as providing plenty of recipes that naturally are dairy-free and/or gluten-free, as well as some vegan recipes, I have also included DF/GF/VG next to recipes that can easily be altered to become so. The other recipes, in my opinion, won't work as well with dietary substitutes and therefore haven't been tested using them.

Microwave ovens

It's difficult to tell what microwave oven you will be using as many have different wattages. With short bursts in the microwave to melt something like butter, it doesn't have to be a specific temperature/power level, however, with something like the microwave pudding recipes (pages 158 and 159), it does. These are the wattages of my microwave:

Low: 100–400W
Medium: 400–500W
High: 800–1000W

Baking paper

I refer to baking paper in the recipes, which is also known as baking parchment. This is perfect to bake on as it is non-stick. However, please don't try to bake with greaseproof paper instead, as it's not treated with a non-stick coating and is usually only used for storing food.

Lining tins

Unless there's a specific method mentioned to line the tin in a recipe (like in the Bundt recipe on page 36), this is how I generally do it:

For a round tin – brush a little melted butter around the whole inside of the tin, or if you're using margarine, get a little bit of it on some kitchen paper and lightly wipe it around the tin. Cut out a circle of baking paper the same size as the base of the tin and place it inside the tin at the bottom, making sure none goes up the sides.

For a loaf and square tin – brush a little melted butter around the whole inside of the tin, or if you're using margarine, get a little bit of it on some kitchen paper and lightly wipe it around the tin. Cut two strips of baking paper the same width as both sides of the tin, then place them into the tin, so that they're overlapping. This will help you to lift the bake out of the tin.

Most of the tins are a standard size and depth, however, if there is any specific depth to the tin that is important to the recipe's outcome, it will be specified.

THERE'S ALWAYS AN OCCASION TO BAKE

Baking (and showing people you care enough to turn the oven on and spend some time in the kitchen) has been incredibly helpful in certain situations. I thought it would be fun to go through some specific occasions you may encounter and what I would suggest baking for them:

If you…

- Are looking for something impressive to bake for the new in-laws to make them forget about your partner's ex. *(Brown Sugar Pavlova, page 102)*

- Have moved to a new place and want to have an excuse to say hello to your neighbours instead of leaving it a year and awkwardly smiling at them while putting the bins out. *(Paloma Marmalade, page 70)*

- Have been watching a lot of the Great British Bake Off and figured 'how hard could it really be?'. *(Beignets, page 30)*

- Want to impress your parents with a killer dessert so it diverts the conversation and takes the pressure off the fact that you haven't bought a house or aren't married. *(Mocha Self-saucing Pudding, page 156)*

- Have been asked to bring a cake to a bake sale and don't want to be the only parent to have bought something from a supermarket on the way to school. *(Jammy Dodgers, page 136)*

- Want to whip up a bake for extra comfort after you embarrassed yourself at a work Christmas party and have woken up with beer fear. *(Hungover Sausage Sarnie Pasties, page 125)*

- Should probably bring some cookies to a neighbour because your party was too loud last night. *(Mocha Chocolate Chip Cookies, page 60)*

- Want the comfort from a school dinner's pudding, but how you *remember* it tasting, not how it probably *actually* tasted. *(Lighter Jam Roly-poly, page 135)*

- Spent all your money on renting in London and need to bake all your friends birthday gifts this year as you can't afford to even look at a shop. *(White Chocolate and Ginger Nuts, page 58)*

- Need something to whip up for date night because you've been spending too many hours at the office and haven't seen them in a few weeks. *(Speedy Tiramisu for Two, page 144)*

- Realized it's raining and you don't want to go to the shops but need something sweet using things from your cupboard. *(Speedy Oat and Raisin Cookies, page 84)*

- You have a house full of 50 or so screaming, precocious (sorry, I meant precious) children for your sweet cherub's birthday and need to make a cake to put in goody bags that will eventually be wrapped and stuck to a napkin anyway. *(Gooey Chocolate Traybake, page 32)*

- Have got to bring a cake to the village bake sale that's better than all the cakes, but the village chairman says you must make sure it's not too impressive as you've outshined a lot of the residents and their sad little Victoria sponges. *(Sticky Ginger and Rum Cake, page 21)*.

- Feel The Ritz is too expensive, and you just want a cup of English breakfast tea and a good scone. *(Ultimate Scones, page 63)*

- Saw someone on the internet make a fluffy strawberry cake in some ridiculously unrealistic, stunning, light airy kitchen on a marble counter, with strawberries picked from their allotment, so now you can't stop thinking about it and want to attempt it. *(Strawberry and Lemon Cake, page 23)*

- JUST WANT TO. *(Salted Flapjack Brownie Tart, page 111)*

CELEBRATIONS

This is where the phrase 'I'll bake' comes into its own. Whether you're trying to win over your in-laws, never want to enter a party empty-handed or are trying to impress a certain someone at the event (Who, me? Never…), then these cakes are for you. There are varying skill levels, so there's something for when you're super busy and need to make it late the night before (shout out to all you midnight bakers), or if you have a little more time to bake something elevated but still simple to make.

CELEBRATE GOOD TIMES

Surprisingly, there are many people who would prefer a savoury birthday cake! This is where this idea came from and it's an absolute showstopper. The buttery scone is packed with chives and served with a whipped cream cheese and chutney filling.

GIANT SAVOURY SCONE WITH WHIPPED CREAM CHEESE

SERVES 8
PREP 30 mins, plus cooling
COOK 40 mins

For the scone

475g/1lb 1oz/3½ cups self-raising flour, plus extra for dusting
2 tbsp cornflour
½ tsp fine sea salt
2 tbsp caster sugar
25g/1oz fresh chives, finely chopped
1½ tsp baking powder
125g/4½ oz/generous ½ cup unsalted butter, cold and cubed, plus extra for greasing
1 egg (60g/2¼oz), plus an extra beaten egg, to glaze
180ml/6fl oz/¾ cup milk

For the filling

400g/14oz/1¾ cups cream cheese
¼ tsp dried chilli flakes (optional)
1 small garlic clove, crushed
200g/7oz chutney of your choice
sea salt and freshly ground black pepper

1 Preheat the oven to 200°C/180°C fan/gas 6. Grease an 18cm/7in loose-based round cake tin with butter and line the base with baking paper. For the scone, mix together the flour, cornflour, salt, sugar, chives and baking powder in a large bowl. Rub in the butter with your fingertips until you have a sandy mixture (or you can do this with a few pulses in a food processor).

2 Whisk the egg and milk together, then gradually pour it into the rubbed-in mixture (you may not need it all), mixing with your hands, until you have a soft but not sticky dough. Dust your work surface with flour, tip the dough out onto the work surface and knead until the dough is smooth. Roll the dough into a ball and press down to make an 18cm/7in circle. Place it in the lined cake tin and press down so it evenly fills the tin. Brush the top with the beaten egg to glaze, making sure it doesn't drip down the sides as it will affect the rise. Bake for 35–40 minutes until risen and golden.

3 Meanwhile, prepare the filling. Beat together the cream cheese, a pinch of salt, a crack of black pepper, the chilli flakes, if using, and garlic in a bowl with an electric whisk or in a stand mixer for 5 minutes until creamy and smooth. Set aside.

4 Remove the baked scone from the oven, cool in the tin for 5 minutes, then remove and transfer to a wire rack to cool completely. Using a serrated knife, carefully slice the scone in half horizontally through the middle.

5 Place the bottom half of the scone on your serving plate, spoon over the cream cheese filling in an even layer, top with the chutney and place the lid of the scone on top. Serve in slices. Store in an airtight container (or covered) in the fridge for up to 3 days.

This nutty, crunchy caramel cake is one for those of you who want something a bit different to your regular sponge and buttercream. The praline is simple to make in a food processor and you use it for both the cream and decoration, adding the best toasty nutty flavour and crunchy texture. The cake is also simple to decorate (and travel with) as it's covered in the beautiful, caramelized nuts.

PRALINE CRUNCH CAKE

SERVES 10–12
PREP 45 mins, plus cooling
COOK 25 mins

For the praline and filling

150g/5½oz/¾ cup caster or granulated sugar
125g/4½oz/1 cup blanched hazelnuts, almonds or pecans or a mixture, toasted
1 tsp fine sea salt
1 tsp vegetable or olive oil
600ml/1 pint/2½ cups double cream
2 tbsp soft dark brown sugar

For the sponge

250g/9oz/generous 1 cup unsalted butter, softened, or margarine, plus extra for greasing
125g/4½oz/⅔ cup caster sugar
125g/4½oz/⅔ cup soft dark brown sugar
4 eggs
250g/9oz/scant 2 cups self-raising flour
1 tsp baking powder
2 tbsp milk

1 First make the praline. Line a baking tray with baking paper. Put 100g/3½oz/½ cup of the caster or granulated sugar in a large frying pan over a medium heat for up to 8 minutes until it melts, stirring occasionally once it has started to melt. When it's runny and starts to caramelize and turn a deep amber, stir in the nuts. Pour onto the baking paper, spread out, sprinkle with the salt and leave to cool completely.

2 Preheat the oven to 180°C/160°C fan/gas 4. Grease two 20cm/8in round sandwich cake tins with butter or margarine and line the bases with baking paper. For the sponge, beat together the butter or margarine and both sugars in a bowl using an electric whisk until light and fluffy. Gradually add in the eggs, then fold in the flour, baking powder and milk until you have a smooth batter. Divide evenly between the two lined tins and spread level using a spatula. Bake for 22–25 minutes until golden and a skewer inserted into the centre comes out clean.

3 Turn out onto a wire rack and cool completely. Meanwhile, finish the filling. Break up the cooled praline into pieces and place in a food processor or mini chopper, then blitz in a few pulses until you have a rough, crumbly mixture. Remove half of it and set aside. Add in the oil to the rest and continue to blitz for 2 minutes until you get a paste.

continues…

4   Whisk together the cream, praline paste and brown sugar in a bowl using an electric whisk until you have soft peaks, being careful not to over-whip.

5   Before assembling, if you need to, trim the top of the cake with a sharp serrated knife so that it's level. To assemble, put one sponge onto a cake board or plate and spread a third of the cream mix over the middle, then sprinkle over a third of the praline crumble. Place the other sponge on top, then spread the remaining cream mix all over the cake, smoothing it around the sides and top using a palette knife (this doesn't need to be perfect). Finish it off by sprinkling the remaining praline crumble all over the top and pressing it around the sides to cover. Serve in slices. Store in an airtight container (or covered) in the fridge for up to 4 days.

TIP To clean the pan to remove any caramel that's left, fill it with water and place over a medium heat until the caramel has dissolved, then wash as usual.

A simple, sticky ginger cake packed full of treacle and stem ginger is my favourite thing to eat when I need something warming on a cold day, or need a quick cake to bring to a bake sale or celebration. It's also delicious eaten warm with some vanilla ice cream.

STICKY GINGER & RUM CAKE

SERVES 8–10
PREP 10 mins, plus cooling
COOK 1 hour

For the sponge

125ml/4fl oz/½ cup vegetable
   oil, plus extra for greasing
80g/3oz (drained weight)
   preserved stem ginger
   balls, drained and very
   finely chopped
70g/2½oz black treacle
300g/10½oz/2½ cups
   self-raising flour
150g/5½oz/¾ cup soft dark
   brown sugar
1 tbsp ground ginger
1 tsp baking powder
a pinch of fine sea salt

For the rum drizzle

40g/1½oz/3¼ tbsp soft dark
   brown sugar
80ml/2½fl oz/5 tbsp dark rum
1 tsp vanilla paste
2 tbsp syrup from the stem
   ginger jar
icing sugar, to serve (optional)

1 Preheat the oven to 180°C/160°C fan/gas 4. Oil a 900g/2lb loaf tin (about 29 x 15.5 x 7.5cm/11½ x 6 x 3in) and line with a strip of baking paper (or use a loaf tin liner). For the sponge, put the oil, 150ml/5fl oz/⅔ cup of water, the stem ginger and black treacle into a large jug and whisk together.

2 Tip the flour, brown sugar, ginger, baking powder and salt into a large bowl and gradually stir in the wet ingredients until you have a smooth batter. Tip into the lined tin and level with the back of a spoon. Bake for 55 minutes–1 hour until a deep brown colour and a skewer inserted into the centre comes out clean.

3 When the sponge has 5 minutes of cooking time left, make the rum drizzle. Put the brown sugar, rum, vanilla and stem ginger syrup into a saucepan over a medium heat, whisk until the sugar has dissolved, then immediately turn off the heat (we're not looking to make a thick syrup).

4 Remove the cake from the oven. Use a skewer to poke small holes into the top of the hot cake. Pour over the warm drizzle, then leave the cake in the tin to cool completely.

5 Turn out and dust the cake with icing sugar, if you like. Serve in slices. Keep in an airtight container (or wrapped) for up to 4 days.

Strawberries and cream are a classic, and when combined with a little lemon, you have a winner. I've made the most of the strawberries by putting them in the sponge for extra moisture, and this, combined with a swirl of lemon curd in the whipped cream, takes this cake to the next level.

STRAWBERRY & LEMON CAKE

SERVES 8–10
PREP 45 mins, plus cooling
COOK 40 mins

For the sponge

225g/8oz/1 cup unsalted butter, softened, or margarine, plus extra for greasing
225g/8oz/generous 1 cup caster sugar
1 tsp vanilla paste
4 eggs
225g/8oz/1¾ cups self-raising flour
1 tsp baking powder
grated zest of 2 lemons
200g/7oz fresh strawberries, hulled and cut into 1cm/½in dice

For the icing and decoration

600ml/1 pint/2½ cups double cream
1 tsp vanilla paste
3 tbsp caster sugar
175g/6oz lemon curd
200g/7oz fresh strawberries, hulled and halved (some with hulls left on)

1 Preheat the oven to 180°C/160°C fan/gas 4 and grease two 18cm/7in round sandwich cake tins with butter or margarine and line the bases with baking paper. In a bowl, beat together the butter or margarine, sugar and vanilla with an electric whisk for up to 7 minutes until light and fluffy, then gradually beat in the eggs. Fold in the flour and baking powder until combined, then fold in the lemon zest and diced strawberries. Divide the mixture evenly between the two lined tins and level with the back of a spoon.

2 Bake for 35–40 minutes until a skewer inserted into the centre comes out clean and the sponge is golden. Run a small, sharp knife around the edges of the tins. Cool in the tins for 5 minutes, then turn out onto a wire rack, top-side facing down (this will give it a flatter top), and cool completely.

3 For the icing, put the cream, vanilla and sugar into a bowl and whisk with an electric whisk (or by hand if you're feeling strong) until it's just starting to thicken and hold its shape. If you have a piping bag fitted with a star nozzle, put the cream into it (this isn't essential).

4 Place one sponge on your serving plate, pipe some of the cream icing around the top edge of the sponge using an up and down motion to look like waves. If you don't have a piping bag, you don't have to pipe around the edges. Spoon a few more spoonfuls of cream icing into the middle of the sponge and smooth with the back of a spoon. Swirl in half the lemon curd and press in half the strawberries (without hulls).

5 Sandwich the other sponge on top and continue with the wavy piping, covering the top of the cake with the remaining cream icing (or just spread it over). Dot over the rest of the lemon curd, then top with the remaining strawberries (with hulls). Slice and serve. Store in an airtight container (or covered) in the fridge for up to 3 days.

TIP Once baked (end of step 2), you can freeze the cooled sponge cakes for up to 2 months, then defrost and continue from step 3.

Sometimes, okay often, I can't be bothered or don't have time to decorate elaborate cakes, which is how this decoration came about. You don't need to pipe or even be good at putting icing on the sides of the cake because that's all hidden with the biscuit mosaic. It also adds a bit of texture to the cake and looks deceptively impressive.

MOSAIC BISCUIT TIN CAKE

SERVES 8–10
PREP 40 mins, plus cooling
COOK 35 mins

For the cake

350g/12oz/2⅔ cups
self-raising flour
a pinch of fine sea salt
225g/8oz/generous 1 cup
caster sugar
½ tsp bicarbonate of soda
150ml/5fl oz/⅔ cup vegetable
oil, plus extra for greasing
2 tsp vanilla paste
½ tbsp white wine vinegar
or apple cider vinegar

For the icing and decoration

200g/7oz/generous
¾ cup unsalted butter
(or dairy-free butter/
spread), softened
400g/14oz/scant 3 cups icing
sugar
3 tbsp milk (regular or
plant-based)
1 tsp vanilla paste
300g/10½oz biscuits (vegan
or dairy free, if needed), a
quarter roughly chopped
and the rest sliced in half
through the middle if
filled (I used a mixture of
bourbons, custard creams,
party rings and jammy
dodgers)

1   Preheat the oven to 180°C/160°C fan/gas 4. Grease two 18cm/7in round sandwich cake tins with oil and line the bases with baking paper. For the cake, add the flour, salt, sugar and bicarb into a large bowl. Gradually whisk in the oil, vanilla, vinegar and 250ml/9fl oz/ generous 1 cup of water until you have a smooth batter.

2   Tip the batter into the two lined tins, dividing it evenly, and level using the back of a spoon. Bake for 30–35 minutes until golden and a skewer inserted into the centre comes out clean. Cool in the tin for 5 minutes, then invert onto a wire rack, top-sides facing down (this will help them flatten if they have risen in the middle) and cool completely.

3   Meanwhile, make the icing. Using an electric whisk or stand mixer (or a wooden spoon and some muscle) beat together the butter and icing sugar in a bowl until pale and smooth. Beat in the milk and vanilla. Set aside.

4   Take one of the sponges and place on a plate or cake board, spoon half of the icing into the middle and spread out evenly. Make a dip in the middle by using a spoon or palette knife and dragging some of the icing outwards. Put the chopped biscuits in the middle and press into the icing. Place the other sponge on top.

5   Spread the rest of the icing around the cake, on the sides and the top, using a palette knife in swiping actions. It doesn't need to be neat as it'll be covered. Take the remaining biscuits and press them onto the sides of the cake, breaking up some to fit in the gaps, so that the sides and the top are covered in a mosaic of biscuits. Store in an airtight container (or wrapped) for up to 3 days.

I promise this cake sounds far more pretentious than it is! The plums roast at the same time as your cakes cook and the cake mix is an all-in-one method. Simple, yet your friends will think you spent hours making it for their birthday – a win-win.

ROASTED PLUM CAKE WITH CREAM CHEESE FROSTING

SERVES 8–10
PREP 35 mins, plus cooling
COOK 30 mins

For the plums

grated zest and juice of
   1 lemon
2 tbsp runny honey, plus
   (optional) extra to serve
7–8 ripe plums, halved and
   stoned (if you can't find
   ripe ones, bake them for
   5 minutes longer)

For the sponge

250g/9oz/generous 1 cup
   unsalted butter, very soft,
   plus extra for greasing
250g/9oz/1¼ cups caster sugar
1 tsp vanilla paste or extract
4 eggs
250g/9oz/scant 2 cups
   self-raising flour
1 tsp baking powder
100g/3½oz/scant ½ cup
   full-fat natural yogurt

For the cream cheese frosting

150g/5½oz/⅔ cup unsalted
   butter, softened
150g/5½oz/1 cup icing sugar,
   sifted
1 tsp vanilla paste or extract
300g/10½oz/1⅓ cups full-fat
   cream cheese

1 Preheat the oven to 180°C/160°C fan/gas 4. Grease two 20cm/8in round sandwich cake tins with butter and line the bases with baking paper. For the plums, mix the lemon zest and juice with the honey and pour over the plums in a bowl, mixing until they're coated, then place them, cut-side up on a baking tray. Set aside.

2 Put all the sponge ingredients into a large bowl and whisk together with an electric whisk until smooth and combined. Divide evenly between the two lined tins, using the back of a spoon to level. Put the cake tins and tray of plums into the oven (plums should be on the bottom shelf) and bake for 25–30 minutes until the cakes are golden and a skewer inserted into the centre comes out clean, and the plums are soft.

3 Remove both from the oven, then turn the cakes out onto a wire rack and cool completely. Trim a little off the top of the sponge with a sharp serrated knife if needed, to make level. Let the plums cool, too, then roughly chop half of them and leave the rest as they are (or cut them in half, or do a mixture as here) for decoration on the top of the cake.

4 Meanwhile, make the frosting. Beat together the butter, icing sugar and vanilla in a bowl with an electric whisk (or a wooden spoon and some muscle) for around 4 minutes until pale and fluffy. Beat the cream cheese in a separate bowl to loosen, then add into the frosting and whisk for 4 minutes until pale. Spread half of the frosting over one of your sponges, then press the chopped plums over the frosting. Put the other sponge on top and swirl over the remaining frosting.

5 Arrange the halved and/or quartered plums on top and drizzle with some extra honey to finish, if you like. Serve in slices. Store in an airtight container (or covered) in the fridge for up to 3 days.

This zingy fresh cake is one I turn to when I don't have the time to ice a whole cake for someone's birthday. It feels luxe and decadent without having to spend ages concentrating over a turntable.

LEMON & OLIVE OIL DRIZZLE CAKE

SERVES 10
PREP 15 mins
COOK 1 hour 10 mins

For the cake
200g/7oz/scant 1 cup full-fat natural yogurt
grated zest of 4 lemons
3 eggs
250g/9oz/1¼ cups caster sugar
200ml/7fl oz/generous ¾ cup olive oil (or you can use vegetable oil), plus extra for greasing
200g/7oz/1⅓ cups polenta
100g/3½oz/1 cup ground almonds
a pinch of fine sea salt
½ tsp bicarbonate of soda
½ tsp baking powder (gluten free, if needed)

For the drizzle syrup
juice of 3 lemons
50g/1¾oz/¼ cup caster sugar

To serve
1 tbsp icing sugar
dollops of full-fat natural yogurt

1 Preheat the oven to 180°C/160°C fan/gas 4. Grease a 23cm/9in deep round (springform) cake tin with oil and line the base with baking paper.

2 For the cake, whisk together the yogurt, lemon zest, eggs, sugar and olive oil in a large bowl. Tip in the polenta, ground almonds, salt, bicarb and baking powder and stir until everything is combined. Don't worry, the mixture will be runny. Pour into the lined tin and level with the back of a spoon. Bake for 1 hour–1 hour 10 minutes until golden and a skewer inserted into the centre comes out clean. You can cover the top with foil after 35 minutes if it starts to colour too much.

3 Leave to cool slightly in the tin while you make the drizzle syrup. Put the lemon juice, sugar and 2 tablespoons of water into a small pan and bring to the boil, stirring until the sugar dissolves, then take off the heat. Using a skewer, poke holes into the warm cake and evenly pour over the syrup.

4 Remove from the tin – you can leave it to cool completely on a wire rack or serve it warm. To serve, dust with the icing sugar and serve in slices with natural yogurt dolloped on the side. Store in an airtight container (or covered) for up to 4 days.

This is one of my favourite ways to use up leftover bananas, when you're not in the mood for banana bread. The buttery biscuit base combined with the toasty salted caramel, creamy bananas and a drizzle of rich chocolate is a dream and a favourite in my family.

BANOFFEE SHORTBREAD SLICES

SERVES 8–10
PREP 35 mins, plus chilling and setting
COOK 10 mins

For the base

225g/8oz shortbread or digestive biscuits
115g/4oz/½ cup unsalted butter, melted, plus extra for greasing

For the caramel

1 x 397g/14oz can Carnation Caramel
75g/2¾oz/⅓ cup unsalted butter, cubed
75g/2¾oz/generous ⅓ cup caster sugar
½ tsp fine sea salt

For the banoffee

300ml/10fl oz/1¼ cups double cream
2 tbsp caster sugar
4–5 small ripe bananas (500g/1lb 2oz unpeeled weight), finely sliced

For the topping

50g/1¾oz dark chocolate, melted and cooled slightly

1 Grease the base of a 20cm/8in loose-based round cake tin with a little butter and line with baking paper, ensuring the butter remains under the paper and not on top (otherwise the shortbread will stick). For the base, crush the biscuits – either blitz them in a food processor or put them in a ziplock bag and whack them with a rolling pin. Tip into a bowl and mix with the melted butter, then press evenly into the base of the lined tin using the back of a spoon. Refrigerate for 15 minutes, until it's set slightly.

2 Meanwhile, make the caramel. Put the Carnation Caramel, butter and sugar into a saucepan over a medium heat and stir occasionally until melted together. Turn the heat to low-medium and simmer for 8–10 minutes until it has turned a darker golden brown and thickened slightly. (To be technical, it should be around 115°C, but don't worry if you don't have a thermometer, just set a timer for 9 minutes and look at the colour and thickness to tell.) Stir in the salt, then pour the caramel over the biscuit base and chill in the fridge for 30 minutes so the caramel cools and sets slightly.

3 For the banoffee, whip the cream with the sugar until it's thick enough to hold its shape, then stir in the bananas. Tip the cream mixture on top of the cooled caramel and spread out in an even layer.

4 Drizzle the melted chocolate in a circular motion on top of the cream, or you can spread it over the whole top to look more like a millionaire slice. Chill in the fridge for 2 hours to set completely. To remove from the tin, dunk a small, sharp knife into a jug of boiling water, wipe dry, then run it around the edge of the tin to release it. Remove from the tin and cut into slices to serve. Store in an airtight container (or covered) in the fridge for up to 3 days.

Beignets are basically square-shaped doughnuts with a fluffy, airy centre. They are synonymous with New Orleans (they have famously been sold in Café Du Monde since 1862, but they were brought to New Orleans by the French in the 18th century), so I've tried to pay homage to their origins. These fluffy, golden beignets covered in icing sugar are delicious eaten warm and dunked in The Perfect Chocolate Sauce on page 47.

BEIGNETS

MAKES around 20
PREP 30 mins, plus 2 hours proving
COOK 12 mins (in batches)

100ml/3½fl oz/generous ⅓ cup milk
30g/1oz/2 tbsp unsalted butter, cut into small cubes
70ml/2½fl oz/scant 5 tbsp boiling water
325g/11½oz/2⅓ cups strong white bread flour, plus extra for dusting
1 x 7g/⅙oz sachet easy-blend dried yeast
30g/1oz/2½ tbsp caster sugar
½ tsp fine sea salt
1–1.5 litres/1¾–2¾ pints/ generous 4 cups–generous 6 cups vegetable or rapeseed oil, for deep-frying
50g/1¾oz/generous ⅓ cup icing sugar

1   Start by making the dough. Put the milk and butter into a large bowl and pour over the boiling water, leave until the butter has melted, then stir. Set the mixture aside to cool until it's lukewarm.

2   Put the flour into a separate bowl, mix the yeast and caster sugar into one side of the flour and the salt into the other side, then mix everything together (this stops the salt from killing the yeast). Gradually tip the melted butter mixture into the flour mixture (you may not need it all), mixing as you go, then knead together with your hands to make a dough. Lightly flour your work surface and knead the dough by hand for 8 minutes, or in a stand mixer with a dough hook for 5 minutes, until you have a smooth dough that springs back when pressed. Place in a clean bowl, cover with a clean tea towel and leave in a warm place for up to 2 hours until doubled in size.

3   Lightly flour your work surface and roll out the dough into an 8mm/ ³⁄₈in-thick rectangle that's around 20 x 27cm/8 x 10¾in, then cut into squares that are approximately 6cm/2½in in size (you should get about 20).

4   Pour the oil into a heavy-based saucepan so it's around half-full. Heat the oil to 175°C or until a small piece of dough dropped into the oil bubbles and turns golden within 30 seconds. Line a plate with some kitchen paper and get a wire rack ready.

5   Working in batches so they don't stick together, deep-fry the dough squares for 1–2 minutes on each side until golden and puffed up. Remove with a slotted spoon or spider strainer, place on the kitchen paper, then transfer to the wire rack and keep warm. Repeat with the remaining dough squares, making sure the oil is up to temperature before adding the next batch. Dust the beignets heavily with the icing sugar and enjoy them warm. Keep in an airtight container for up to 2 days.

This is the ultimate gooey rich chocolate traybake, it's simple to put together, the icing can be made in minutes and it will always impress. I brought a tray of this to my friend Connor's birthday party and it was demolished as people went back for third portions – it's the perfect nostalgic comforting cake.

GOOEY CHOCOLATE TRAYBAKE

SERVES 10–12
PREP 20 mins, plus cooling
COOK 40 mins

For the chocolate sponge

200g/7oz/scant 1 cup full-fat
  Greek yogurt
juice of ½ lemon
150ml/5fl oz/⅔ cup vegetable
  oil, plus extra for greasing
200ml/7fl oz/generous ¾ cup
  strong brewed coffee,
  cooled slightly
2 eggs
1 tsp vanilla paste
250g/9oz/scant 2 cups self-
  raising flour
75g/2¾oz/¾ cup
  unsweetened cocoa
  powder
1 tsp bicarbonate of soda
150g/5½oz/¾ cup caster
  sugar
150g/5½oz/¾ cup soft light
  brown sugar
2 tsp sea salt flakes

For the icing

100g/3½oz dark chocolate,
  melted
100g/3½oz/scant ½ cup
  unsalted butter, melted
200g/7oz/scant 1½ cups icing
  sugar, sifted
2 tbsp unsweetened cocoa
  powder
2 tsp sea salt flakes

1 Preheat the oven to 180°C/160°C fan/gas 4 and grease a 35 x 25cm/ 14 x 10in deep baking tin or casserole dish with oil, then line with two strips of baking paper (overhanging the ends of the tin/dish for easy removal). For the sponge, stir the yogurt and lemon juice together and leave to sit for 2 minutes. Put the vegetable oil, coffee, eggs, vanilla and yogurt mixture into a jug and whisk together.

2 Tip the flour, cocoa powder, bicarb, caster and brown sugars and the salt flakes into a large bowl and rub through your fingers to combine and break up the brown sugar. Mix the wet ingredients into the dry until you have a smooth, thin batter. Pour into the prepared tin or dish, level with the back of a spoon, then bake for 35–40 minutes until risen and a skewer inserted into the centre comes out clean. Leave to cool completely in the tin.

3 Put all the icing ingredients, except the salt flakes, in a bowl and stir in 75ml/2½fl oz/5 tbsp of water until you get a smooth, thin icing. Pour evenly on top of your cooled cake and then leave for around 30 minutes until set. Remove from the tin, sprinkle with the salt flakes and cut into squares. Store in an airtight container for up to 3 days.

TIP You can use 200ml/7fl oz/generous ¾ cup of buttermilk instead of the yogurt and lemon juice, if you have any.

CELEBRATIONS

This is the perfect bake for around Christmastime, or if you happen to have discovered a leftover jar of mincemeat during the year. Super simple as you don't have to blind bake it first, and it will be the perfect thing to eat with a cup of tea.

FRANGIPANE FESTIVE TART

SERVES 8
PREP 20 mins, plus cooling
COOK 55 mins

1 x 320g/11½oz ready-rolled
    puff pastry sheet
250g/9oz/generous 1 cup
    mincemeat

For the frangipane

125g/4½oz/⅔ cup caster sugar
125g/4½oz/generous ½ cup
    unsalted butter, softened
2 eggs
75g/2¾oz/generous ½ cup
    plain flour
125g/4½oz/1¼ cups ground
    almonds
1½ tsp baking powder
2 tbsp flaked almonds
1 tbsp icing sugar (optional)

1 Preheat the oven to 190°C/170°C fan/gas 5 and put a large, flat baking sheet in the oven to heat up. Unroll the pastry and press it into a 20cm/8in loose-based deep round cake tin (4cm/1½in deep) or a 23cm/9in fluted tart tin. Press it into the corners and up the sides so there's a 1–2cm/½–¾in overhang, patching up any areas you need to. Spread the mincemeat over the bottom of the pastry in an even layer.

2 To make the frangipane, beat together the sugar and butter in a bowl using an electric whisk if you have one (or by hand) until pale and fluffy, then beat in 1 egg at a time until everything is combined. Fold in the flour, ground almonds and baking powder until you have a smooth batter. Pour on top of the mincemeat and spread out evenly. Sprinkle the flaked almonds on top.

3 Place the tin on the hot baking sheet in the oven and bake for 50–55 minutes until the frangipane is golden and a skewer inserted into the centre comes out clean. You can cover the top with foil after 25 minutes if it's getting too dark.

4 Cool in the tin for 5 minutes, then remove from the tin and slide onto a wire rack to cool completely. Trim the overhanging baked pastry with a small, sharp knife to neaten the edges, then dust with icing sugar, if you like, and slice. Keep in an airtight container for up to 4 days.

TIP Heating the baking sheet prevents the finished tart from having a soggy bottom.

Nothing says comfort like a slice of tangy but sweet cherry pie slathered in cream. I've taken the classic cherry pie and given it a twist by adding in dark chocolate chunks and a splash of almond extract, so it's similar to a Black Forest gâteau. It's baked for around 2 hours, so the cherries cook down, the chocolatey sauce thickens and the pastry crisps up nicely. If you can't find any frozen cherries, you can use a frozen 'fruits of the forest' mix instead.

BLACK FOREST CHERRY PIE

SERVES 8
PREP 40 mins
COOK 2 hours

700g/1lb 9oz frozen pitted
  sweet cherries
150g/5½oz/¾ cup caster
  or granulated sugar
2 tbsp cornflour
2 tbsp unsweetened cocoa
  powder
¼ tsp almond extract
  (optional)
plain flour, for dusting
500g/1lb 2oz ready-made
  shortcrust pastry
100g/3½oz dark chocolate,
  roughly chopped (or use
  chocolate chips)
1 egg, beaten
2 tbsp demerara sugar
  (optional)
double or single cream,
  to serve

1 Preheat the oven to 200°C/180°C fan/gas 6. Put the frozen cherries, caster or granulated sugar, cornflour, cocoa powder and almond extract, if using, into a large bowl and mix so the cherries are coated.

2 Dust your work surface with some flour and roll out half the pastry so it's slightly bigger than a 26cm/10½in pie dish. Roll the pastry over the rolling pin and then drape it over the dish. Press it into the corners so the dish is lined with pastry, then cut away any excess on the sides.

3 Place a large, flat baking sheet in the oven to heat up. Pour the coated cherries into the lined pie dish and sprinkle over the dark chocolate. Brush the edges of the pastry with egg wash.

4 Sprinkle a little more flour onto your work surface and roll out the remaining pastry to a 26cm/10½in circle, about 0.5cm/¼in thick. Cut into 3cm/1¼in strips for the lattice top. To make the lattice top, weave the strips of pastry under and over each other to cover the filling – you'll have around 4 strips lying vertically and around 4 strips lying horizontally over the filling – lifting and weaving the strips as you go. Trim, then crimp the edges of the pastry to seal them together.

5 Brush the pastry with egg wash and sprinkle over the demerara sugar, if using (this will make it extra golden). Slide the dish onto the hot baking sheet (so the base becomes crisp). Bake for 30 minutes until golden brown, then turn the oven down to 170°C/150°C fan/gas 3 and bake for a further 1½ hours until dark brown and the cherries are bubbling. Leave to cool for 15 minutes, then serve warm in slices, or cool completely and serve at room temperature. Serve with cream. Keep in an airtight container (or covered) in the fridge for up to 4 days.

A traditional cake in my family was a Gugelhupf. The recipe was passed down from my Austrian great-grandmother to my granddad, Henry, and then to my grandmother, Judi, who made it every birthday until we were old enough to know that Costco chocolate cakes existed. It's usually made just with sultanas, but I like to add the dark chocolate and ginger for an extra kick of flavour. The cornflour helps it to hold its structure in the Bundt tin, too.

DARK CHOCOLATE & GINGER GUGELHUPF

SERVES 10
PREP 30 mins, plus cooling
COOK 55 mins

200g/7oz/1½ cups sultanas
3 black teabags
200ml/7fl oz/generous ¾ cup
    boiling water
200g/7oz/generous ¾ cup
    unsalted butter, softened,
    plus extra for greasing
200g/7oz/scant 1½ cups icing
    sugar
a pinch of fine sea salt
3 eggs
250g/9oz/scant 2 cups
    self-raising flour
3 tbsp cornflour
1 tsp baking powder
75g/2¾oz dark chocolate,
    25g/1oz roughly chopped
    (or use chocolate chips)
    and 50g/1¾oz melted
100g/3½oz (drained weight)
    preserved stem ginger
    balls, drained and finely
    grated, plus 1 extra ball,
    sliced, to decorate
2 tbsp plain flour
edible flowers, to decorate
    (optional)

1   Preheat the oven to 180°C/160°C fan/gas 4. Put the sultanas and teabags in a heatproof bowl and pour over the boiling water, cover and leave to steep and cool while you prepare the rest of the cake.

2   Beat together the butter, icing sugar and salt in a mixing bowl using an electric whisk for 5 minutes until pale and fluffy. Gradually add in the eggs, putting in a tablespoon of the weighed flour if it splits. Fold in the rest of the flour, the cornflour and baking powder until you have a smooth, thick batter.

3   The soaking sultanas should now be at room temperature, but if not, wait until they're cool. Fold them and the soaking liquid into the mixture and then mix the chopped chocolate and grated ginger in, too.

continues…

4 Heavily butter a 22cm/8½in Bundt tin (22 x 22 x 11cm/8½ x 8½ x 4¼in), so that you can see the butter inside the tin, getting it in all the creases. Tip in 2 tbsp of flour, shaking around the whole tin so it covers the sides, and shake out any excess. Tip the cake mix into the tin and level with a spoon. Bake for 50–55 minutes until golden brown or a skewer inserted comes out clean (don't worry if it catches some melted chocolate).

5 Remove from the oven, place a plate on top to cover the top (this helps create steam to release the cake from the tin) and leave to cool for 10 minutes, then flip onto a wire rack. Carefully knock on the top of the tin (using a tea towel so you don't burn yourself) to release the cake. Cool completely and then drizzle the melted chocolate over the top. Put the sliced ginger on top and decorate with some edible flowers, if you have any. Store wrapped or in an airtight container for up to 4 days.

TIP Once baked and rested for 10 minutes, if you can still feel the cake is stuck, turn your cake tin the right way up again. Pour boiling water over a tea towel and squeeze it out (once it's cooled slightly), then lay the damp tea towel over the top of the cake in the tin, place a plate on top of it and the steam should help loosen the cake enough after another 10 minutes.

Banana bread has a special place in my heart, not just because it was one of the main (and only) things my mum baked, but it's one of the first things I ever baked. This couldn't be easier, just mix all the ingredients together and put in the tin. I love the little added touch of placing a halved banana and some pecans on top, as it makes it look professional with very little effort! It is really moreish, and even more so spread with Whipped Espresso Butter (page 46).

TOASTED PECAN BANANA BREAD

SERVES 8
PREP 10 mins, plus cooling
COOK 1 hour 20 mins

5 ripe medium bananas,
    4 mashed (400g/14oz flesh),
    the other sliced lengthways
    down the middle to
    decorate the top
200g/7oz/1½ cups self-raising
    flour
75g/2¾oz/¾ cup porridge
    oats
1 tsp baking powder
1 tsp ground cinnamon
100g/3½oz/½ cup soft light
    brown sugar
100g/3½oz/½ cup caster
    sugar
125g/4½oz/generous ½ cup
    butter, melted and cooled
    slightly, plus extra for
    greasing
100g/3½oz/1 cup pecans (or
    use walnuts or pistachios),
    toasted and roughly
    chopped
2 eggs, beaten
Whipped Espresso Butter
    (page 46), to serve
    (optional)

1   Preheat the oven to 180°C/160°C fan/gas 4. Grease a 900g/2lb loaf tin (about 29 x 15.5 x 7.5cm/11½ x 6 x 3in) with butter and line with baking paper (or use a loaf tin liner). Add all the ingredients, except the sliced banana and 25g/1oz/¼ cup of the pecans, into a large bowl and stir together until smooth and combined.

2   Pour into the lined tin and level the top. Place the two banana halves, cut-side up, across the top of the batter, pressing down slightly, then sprinkle the remaining pecans around the banana. Bake for 1¼ hours–1 hour 20 minutes until a skewer inserted into the centre comes out clean, covering the top with foil towards the end of cooking if it starts to brown too much.

3   Leave to cool completely in the tin. Cut into slices to serve with Whipped Espresso Butter, if you like. Store in an airtight container for up to 4 days.

I created this cheesecake to contain all my favourite things in one rich, chocolatey, creamy baked cheesecake with little bursts of spiced chai salted caramel throughout – yes please! You can use digestives for the base, but I like to use ginger biscuits to add an extra hint of spice. If you prefer a plain chocolate cheesecake, you can omit the caramel, and you also don't have to spice the caramel.

CHOCOLATE & CHAI CARAMEL BAKED CHEESECAKE

SERVES 8–10
PREP 45 mins, plus overnight setting
COOK 1½ hours

For the base

225g/8oz ginger biscuits (you can use gluten-free ones, if you prefer)
115g/4oz/½ cup unsalted butter, melted

For the filling

600g/1lb 5oz/2⅔ cups full-fat cream cheese, at room temperature
4 eggs
150g/5½oz/⅔ cup double cream, at room temperature
150g/5½oz/¾ cup light soft brown sugar
2 tsp fine sea salt
350g/12oz dark chocolate, melted and cooled slightly
1 x 397g/14oz can Carnation Caramel
20 green cardamom pods, seeds removed and crushed
1 tsp ground cinnamon
2 tsp ground ginger
¼ tsp ground cloves
sea salt flakes, to serve (optional)

1   Preheat the oven to 180°C/160°C fan/gas 4 and line the base of a 23cm/9in loose-based (springform) round cake tin with baking paper. For the base, blitz the ginger biscuits in a food processor to make crumbs (or you can smash them with a rolling pin in a ziplock bag). Mix in the melted butter and then press into the bottom of your lined tin with the back of a spoon in an even layer. Place the cake tin into a deep baking tin (which you'll use again later), in case any of the butter leaks, and bake for 12 minutes to prevent a soggy bottom. Remove the cake tin from the baking tin and leave to cool.

2   Make the filling. Using an electric whisk, beat together the cream cheese, eggs, cream, sugar and 1 teaspoon of the salt in a bowl for 1–2 minutes until smooth (it doesn't have to thicken). While you continue to whisk, gradually pour in the melted chocolate until everything is combined.

3   Place the cake tin on a large piece of foil and wrap the foil around the bottom of the tin to prevent any leaking, then place it back into the deep baking tin (used earlier). Pour the cheesecake mixture on top of the biscuit base and spread level.

continues…

4 Put the caramel, the remaining salt, the cardamom, cinnamon, ginger and cloves into a bowl and beat until smooth and combined. Reserve a quarter of this (for decoration) in an airtight container, then swirl the remaining caramel into the cheesecake mixture using a small spoon. Boil the kettle and pour enough hot water into the deep baking tin to come 2.5cm/1in up the sides of the cheesecake tin.

5 Bake for 1¼ hours until the cheesecake has a little wobble in the centre but is set around the edges. Remove from the water bath and take away the foil. Run a small, sharp knife around the edge (this will help it sink more evenly), leave to cool completely in the tin, then refrigerate overnight to set completely. Remove the cheesecake from the tin when you're ready to serve, drizzle with the reserved caramel (mixing in a splash of warm water to loosen if it's too thick), sprinkle with some sea salt flakes, if you like, and slice with a hot knife. Store in an airtight container in the fridge for up to 4 days.

TIPS To line the base perfectly, you can unclip the springform tin, lay the baking paper over the base and clip the ring back into place, so there won't be a lip indent on the cheesecake.

For perfectly neat slices, dip your knife in some boiling water, wipe it dry and then slice the cheesecake.

There's an amazing bakery in London called Brickwood that sells their nutty banana bread with espresso butter, and ever since I heard of this I've been making something similar to slather on just about any baked goods. It works especially well with my Toasted Pecan Banana Bread (see page 41), as the creamy, toasty aromatic butter takes it up a notch.

WHIPPED ESPRESSO BUTTER

MAKES around 150g/5½oz
PREP 10 mins
NO COOK

125g/4½oz/generous ½ cup
    salted butter, softened
3 tbsp soft light brown sugar
1 shot of espresso, cooled,
    or 1½ tsp coffee granules
    dissolved in 2 tbsp hot
    water, cooled

1   Put all the ingredients into a bowl and beat with an electric whisk or in a stand mixer (or with a wooden spoon and some muscle) for 5–8 minutes until light, pale and fluffy. Slather on banana bread, toasted crumpets or hot cross buns. Store in an airtight container for up to 5 days.

GF DF VG

A luscious chocolate sauce that will soon become a staple in your home (I can often be found secretly spooning it into my mouth in a corner of the kitchen). This versatile sweet, rich and salty sauce is simple to make and it's nice and thick, so it will coat puddings.

THE PERFECT CHOCOLATE SAUCE

MAKES around 400ml/
14fl oz/scant 1¾ cups
PREP 2 mins
COOK 5 mins

100g/3½oz dark chocolate,
roughly chopped (vegan
and dairy free if needed)
50g/1¾oz/¼ cup caster sugar
½ tsp fine sea salt
2 tbsp golden syrup
200ml/7fl oz/generous ¾ cup
milk (or plant-based milk
for vegan and dairy free)
1 ½ tbsp unsweetened cocoa
powder
1 tbsp liqueur of your choice,
such as coffee or almond
liqueur (optional)

1 Add all the ingredients to a saucepan and cook over a medium heat, whisking until everything has fully melted and combined, then simmer for up to 5 minutes until you have a thick, smooth, glossy sauce. Serve hot.

2 Cool and store any leftover sauce in an airtight container in the fridge for up to 3 days, then reheat gently in a pan until hot before serving.

AFTERNOON

TEA

Gather your favourite people together and throw an afternoon tea get-together, it's the perfect excuse to bake and throw a party. I always enjoyed the adrenaline-filled atmosphere and intricacy of an afternoon tea service when I worked in top London hotels. Every chef in each kitchen taught me a different trick to make the perfect scone, and when you're making hundreds in one batch, it's important that you get them right the first time, every time. My time working in these kitchens led me to create my Ultimate Scones recipe (page 63). Try combining these with the heavenly Roasted Pineapple and Passion Cake (page 66) or my family's favourite Ploughman's Pinwheels (page 55). I hope, with these recipes, you'll be inspired to create the afternoon tea of your dreams.

KITCHEN DANCE PARTY

Savoury madeleines are the way forward – the ultimate fluffy, umami, cheesy bites. These should definitely have a warning on them, that it's almost impossible to eat just one!

CHEESY MARMITE MADELEINES

MAKES 18–20
PREP 20 mins, plus chilling
COOK 10 mins

40g/1½oz/3 tbsp unsalted butter, cubed, plus extra for greasing
1 tbsp Marmite
2 eggs, separated
75g/2¾oz/⅓ cup full-fat Greek yogurt
125g/4½oz/scant 1 cup plain flour
1 tsp baking powder
50g/1¾oz/½ cup Cheddar cheese, finely grated
a pinch of fine sea salt

1. Melt the butter with the Marmite either in short blasts in a microwave oven on medium or in a small pan. Whisk to combine, then pour into a large bowl and leave to cool.

2. Once cooled, whisk the egg yolks and yogurt into the melted butter and Marmite and then fold in the flour, baking powder, 40g/1½oz/ scant ½ cup of the Cheddar and the salt. Take the whites and whisk in a separate bowl using an electric whisk until you have stiff peaks. Using a spatula, fold the whites into the madeleine mix and chill in the fridge for 1 hour.

3. Preheat the oven to 200°C/180°C fan/gas 6 and grease a 12-hole madeleine tin (mine was around 7 x 4cm/2¾ x 1½in per madeleine shape) with butter. Pipe or spoon the chilled mixture into the buttered moulds so that they are each three-quarters full and level, then sprinkle some of the remaining cheese on top of each one. Unless you have a second madeleine tin, you'll need to bake the mixture in two batches.

4. Bake for 10 minutes until golden brown. Remove from the tin and serve warm. You can eat these cold, too, but I prefer snacking on them warm. Store in an airtight container for up to 4 days.

A few years ago, I was walking around a freezing firework display with my friend Laura, trying to find anything to bring us comfort in the bitter cold. We discovered a stall selling an incredible hog roast roll packed with pork, stuffing and apple sauce, which led me to create these delicious sausage rolls. They're the ultimate comfort snack.

HOG ROAST SAUSAGE ROLLS

MAKES 8
PREP 20 mins
COOK 30 mins

400g/14oz pork sausages (skins removed) or pork sausage meat
50g/1¾oz dried sage and onion stuffing mix
1 tbsp dried thyme
1 x 320g/11½oz ready-rolled puff pastry sheet
100g/3½oz ready-made sweetened apple sauce (I use a chunky kind)
1 egg, beaten, to glaze
1 tsp fennel seeds (optional)
sea salt and freshly ground black pepper

1 Preheat the oven to 200°C/180°C fan/gas 6 and put a large, flat baking sheet in the oven. In a large bowl, put the sausage meat, stuffing mix and thyme along with a big pinch each of salt and pepper and mix with your hands to combine.

2 Lay out the sheet of puff pastry and cut it in half lengthways. Spoon half the apple sauce down the centre of each pastry strip, about 5cm/2in wide. Take half of the sausage meat mixture and shape it into a long log on the centre of one of the puff pastry rectangles, then repeat with the other one.

3 Brush the edges with beaten egg, then roll up and seal with the seam of pastry underneath. Brush all over with more egg, then cut each strip into 4 sausage rolls, leaving the cut edges exposed.

4 Take the hot baking sheet out of the oven (this will prevent a soggy bottom), lay a sheet of baking paper on it and place the sausage rolls onto the paper, about 5cm/2in apart. Sprinkle over the fennel seeds, if using, and bake for 28–30 minutes until golden and cooked through. Serve warm or cold. Store in an airtight container in the fridge for up to 3 days and eat cold or reheat until hot through.

There's a sheer childhood nostalgia that peanut butter brings, so just like back then, these PB&J biscuits are the perfect pick-me-up. They're crumbly, buttery and filled with a sticky sweet jam.

PEANUT BUTTER & JELLY SHORTBREAD

MAKES 10–12
PREP 20 mins, plus cooling
COOK 15 mins

100g/3½oz/scant ½ cup unsalted butter, softened
80g/3oz/scant ½ cup caster sugar
50g/1¾oz/scant ¼ cup peanut butter (I used Manilife deep roast crunchy peanut butter)
150g/5½oz/generous 1 cup plain flour
a pinch of fine sea salt
4 tbsp jam of your choice (I used raspberry)

1 Preheat the oven to 190°C/170°C fan/gas 5 and line a large, flat baking sheet with baking paper. Beat together the butter and sugar in a mixing bowl for 2–3 minutes until you have a smooth, fluffy mixture and then mix in the peanut butter until combined. Tip in the flour along with the salt and mix until you have a smooth dough, adding in up to 1 teaspoon of water to bind, kneading together into a ball.

2 Take golf ball-sized pieces of dough, each around 30g/1oz, and shape each into a ball. Place onto the lined baking sheet and press your thumb into the middle of each one to make a shallow dip in the dough. Fill each dip with around a teaspoon of jam.

3 Bake for 12–15 minutes until golden brown and spread slightly. Leave to cool completely on the baking sheet. Store in an airtight container for up to 3 days.

The perfect alternative to sandwiches for an afternoon tea or picnic, these pinwheels are packed full of things I normally have lying around the fridge, like ham, cheese and a jar of piccalilli. They're great eaten warm or enjoyed cold on a summer's day.

PLOUGHMAN'S PINWHEELS

MAKES 10–12
PREP 10 mins
COOK 25 mins

75g/2¾oz/¾ cup mature Cheddar cheese, grated
125g/4½oz piccalilli, finely chopped if chunky
4 small spring onions, finely sliced
1 x 320g/11½oz ready-rolled puff pastry sheet
5 slices of cooked ham

1 Preheat the oven to 220°C/200°C fan/gas 7 and line a large, flat baking sheet with baking paper. Mix the Cheddar, piccalilli and spring onions together.

2 Unroll the puff pastry onto your work surface and lay over the ham slices, halving some, so the pastry is fully covered but the slices don't go over the sides. Spread the piccalilli mix evenly over the ham.

3 Roll up into a swirl from the longest side and slice into 10–12 slices. With each slice, using your fingertips, gently squeeze the end of the swirl into the pastry to seal and prevent leaking.

4 Place them onto the lined baking sheet, swirl-side facing up, about 5cm/2in apart. Bake for 25 minutes until golden. Cool slightly on the baking sheet, then transfer to a wire rack to cool completely. Serve warm or cold. Keep in an airtight container in the fridge for up to 3 days.

These beauties are a mixture of a ginger snap and a chocolate chip cookie with the texture of a snickerdoodle. They're the perfect sweet spicy snack dunked in a cup of tea, and can be frozen and baked off whenever you fancy one.

WHITE CHOCOLATE & GINGER NUTS

MAKES 18–20
PREP 20 mins, plus cooling
COOK 12 mins

125g/4½oz/generous ½ cup unsalted butter, cubed
a pinch of fine sea salt
70g/2½oz/⅓ cup soft dark brown sugar
70g/2½oz/⅓ cup caster sugar
200g/7oz/1½ cups plain flour
1 tbsp ground ginger
1 tsp bicarbonate of soda
200g/7oz white chocolate, half roughly chopped (or use chocolate chips) and half melted
1½ tbsp milk

1 Preheat the oven to 200°C/180°C fan/gas 6. Line two large baking trays with baking paper. In a large bowl, using an electric whisk, beat together the butter, salt and both sugars until light and fluffy.

2 Tip in the flour, ginger, bicarb and the chopped white chocolate and stir together to make a dough, adding in the milk to loosen the mixture. Take a heaped tablespoonful of the mix (around 30g/1oz, if you want to be accurate), roll into a ball and place on a lined baking tray. Repeat with the rest of the mix, spacing the balls about 8cm/3½in apart as they will spread. Press down slightly so they're each about 1.5cm/⅝in thick.

3 Bake for 10–12 minutes until golden brown. Cool on the baking trays for 5 minutes, then transfer to a wire rack to cool completely. Once cool, using a teaspoon (or a disposable piping bag with the end snipped off, if you want to be precise), drizzle the melted white chocolate in lines across the biscuits. Leave to set before serving. Store in an airtight container for up to 4 days.

TIP You can freeze the balls (on the baking trays) after they've been pressed down but before they've been baked. Once frozen, store in a freezer bag (to save space in the freezer), then return to the baking trays for baking. Bake from frozen at 200°C/180°C fan/gas 6 for 14–15 minutes. Freeze (unbaked) for up to 3 months.

A crisp golden coconut flapjack base with a creamy coconut chocolate filling will impress everyone at the table. My favourite thing about this luxurious tart is that it's not too sweet as the sweetness comes from the dates and maple syrup.

COCONUT CHOCOLATE FLAPJACK TART

MAKES 8–10
PREP 35 mins, plus 20 mins
    soaking, cooling and
    overnight chilling
COOK 20 mins

For the flapjack

6 medjool dates, stoned
vegan/dairy-free spread,
    for greasing
100g/3½oz coconut oil,
    melted
150g/5½oz/1½ cups porridge
    oats (gluten free if needed)
50g/1¾oz/⅔ cup desiccated
    coconut
3 tbsp hot water

For the filling

300g/10½oz dark chocolate,
    roughly chopped (vegan
    and dairy free if needed)
250g/9oz coconut cream
    (not milk)
½ tsp sea salt flakes, plus
    extra for sprinkling
2 tbsp maple or agave syrup
2 tbsp coconut flakes,
    toasted

1   For the flapjack, cover the dates with boiling water and leave for 20 minutes. Preheat the oven to 190°C/170°C fan/gas 5. Grease the base of an 18cm/7in loose-based round cake tin (around 4cm/1½in deep) with a vegan/dairy-free spread and line with baking paper.

2   Drain the dates (discard the soaking water), add to a food processor with the coconut oil and process until you have a paste that's relatively smooth. Mix the paste with the oats, desiccated coconut and hot water. Press the mixture into the base and up the sides of the lined tin with the back of a spoon. Bake for 20 mins until starting to turn golden, then leave to cool completely.

3   To make the filling, put the chocolate into a large, heatproof bowl. Put the coconut cream, ½ teaspoon of the salt flakes and the maple/agave syrup in a saucepan over a medium heat until it starts to boil. Pour this over the chocolate, put a plate over the bowl to lock in the heat, leave to sit for a minute and then stir together until the chocolate melts (if it doesn't melt completely, give it a quick 30-second blast in a microwave oven on medium).

4   Pour the chocolate ganache over the flapjack base, smooth over to level and leave to cool completely. Once cool, refrigerate for 5 hours or overnight to set completely. Remove from the tin, sprinkle with a pinch of salt flakes and the coconut flakes, then slice into wedges with a hot knife to serve. Store in an airtight container for up to 4 days.

These cookies taste like a coffee cake but in gooey, chewy cookie form, with chunks of chocolate. I can't tell you how delicious they are – the best thing is that you can freeze the dough and have cookies whenever you want!

MOCHA CHOCOLATE CHIP COOKIES

MAKES 18–20
PREP 20 mins, plus cooling
COOK 12 mins

125g/4½oz/generous ½ cup unsalted butter, softened
175g/6oz/generous ¾ cup soft light brown sugar
100g/3½oz/½ cup caster sugar
½ tsp sea salt flakes, plus extra for sprinkling
1 egg (55g/2oz – if it's less, make up the quantity with water)
2 tbsp coffee granules mixed with 2 tbsp boiling water (leave to cool slightly) or 2 tbsp espresso (cooled)
1 tsp vanilla paste (optional, if you have some)
300g/10½oz/2¼ cups plain flour
½ tsp baking powder
200g/7oz dark chocolate, chopped into chunks (or use chocolate chips)

1   Preheat the oven to 190°C/170°C fan/gas 5 and line two large baking trays with baking paper or a silicone mat.

2   Beat together the butter, both sugars and sea salt flakes in a large bowl with an electric whisk for 4–5 minutes until creamy, pale and smooth (or beat by hand with a wooden spoon if you're feeling strong). Beat in the egg, coffee and vanilla and mix again (don't worry if it looks split at this stage). Tip in the flour and baking powder and mix until you have a thick, pliable mixture. Fold in the dark chocolate.

3   Take 50g/1¾oz of the mixture (you can weigh each one to be accurate or weigh one and eyeball the rest) and roll it into a ball. Repeat with the rest of the dough.

4   Place onto the prepared baking trays, leaving about 6cm/2½in space between them. With the palm of your hand, gently press down on each one until they're around 1cm/½in thick, then sprinkle with a few sea salt flakes. Once pressed, you can bake them at this point, or cover and keep them in the fridge for up to a week, or in the freezer for up to 3 months.

5   Bake for 10–12 minutes until golden brown. Leave to cool slightly on the baking trays, then transfer to a wire rack and leave to cool completely. Sprinkle with a little extra flaky salt if you like. Tuck in and enjoy! Cook unbaked ones from the fridge for 12–14 minutes and cook from frozen for 13–15 minutes. Store in an airtight container for up to 4 days.

TIP When they come out of the oven and are still hot, you can re-shape each one into a perfect circle. Take a large, flat-edged cookie cutter that is slightly larger than the cookie and move it in a circular motion around the cookie, for a neat circle.

During my years in professional kitchens as a pastry chef, scones were always on the menu for afternoon tea. We made them in several kilo batches at places like The Ritz, so it was important that they baked perfectly every time, and I quickly learnt tips on how to make them consistent. Here is my foolproof recipe. To make it vegan, choose the ingredient options given in brackets below.

ULTIMATE SCONES

MAKES 6–8
PREP 30 mins, plus chilling
COOK 13 mins

425g/15oz/3¼ cups
    self-raising flour, plus
    extra for dusting
¼ tsp fine sea salt
4 tbsp caster sugar
1½ tsp baking powder
125g/4½oz/generous ½ cup
    unsalted butter, cold and
    cubed (or vegan butter)
100g/3½oz/¾ cup sultanas
    (optional)
180ml/6fl oz/¾ cup milk
    (or plant-based milk)
1 egg, beaten, for glazing (or
    use extra plant-based milk)

1 Mix the flour, salt, sugar and baking powder in a large bowl. Rub in the butter with your fingertips until you have a sandy mixture (if you have one, this can be done with a few pulses in a food processor). Mix in the sultanas, if using.

2 Gradually pour in the milk, mixing with your hands, until you have a soft but not sticky dough. Roll out the dough on a sheet of baking paper so it's 2cm/¾in thick. Cover it with another sheet of baking paper and chill in the fridge for 30–40 minutes to firm up slightly and rest (this also helps to make perfect shapes).

3 Preheat the oven to 220°C/200°C fan/gas 7 and line two large, flat baking sheets with baking paper. Using a 7cm/2¾in round cookie cutter, cut as many as you can out of the dough. When cutting, press down in one straight motion, don't twist the cutter or they may rise slanted. Invert each one (so the flat bottom is now at the top) and place on the lined baking sheets about 5cm/2in apart. Re-roll the dough until it's all used up.

4 Brush the tops of the scones with egg wash, making sure none drips down the edges (drips cause them to rise slanted) and bake for 12–13 minutes until risen and golden. Transfer to a wire rack to cool, then serve warm or cold. Store in an airtight container for up to 3 days, or wrap and freeze for up to 2 months, then defrost before serving.

Surprisingly, lemon curd is expensive to make, and it can go wrong quite easily. This is a cheaper alternative that is perfect with scones and foolproof as the cornflour stops it from splitting. I normally make this large quantity to serve with my Ultimate Scones on page 63 and have leftovers to enjoy for breakfast spooned on yogurt, granola or toast. You can halve the quantities if you just want it for the scones.

10-MINUTE CHEAT'S LEMON CURD

MAKES around 800g/ 1lb 12oz
PREP 5 mins, plus cooling
COOK 10 mins

juice of 4–5 large lemons (you need 200ml/7fl oz/ generous ¾ cup juice)
200g/7oz/1 cup caster sugar
4 tbsp cornflour
4 egg yolks
70g/2½oz/⅓ cup unsalted butter, cut into small cubes

1 Put the lemon juice, 200ml/7fl oz/generous ¾ cup of water and the caster sugar into a saucepan over a medium heat and bring to the boil.

2 Meanwhile, add 50ml/2fl oz/3½ tbsp of water to the cornflour in a small bowl and whisk until it's dissolved into the water.

3 Once the lemon mixture is boiling, turn down the heat to low-medium and whisk in the cornflour mixture, continuing to whisk for 2 minutes until it's thickened.

4 Take off the heat and whisk in the egg yolks and then the butter until combined. Transfer into a bowl (or a sterilized screw-top jam jar or two), then leave to cool completely and set. Once cool, cover tightly and store in the fridge for up to 5 days.

TIP To save waste, you can grate the zest of the lemons and freeze it in a small tub or an ice-cube tray for later use.

I love making this speedy compote to add to porridge in the mornings, or it goes perfectly alongside my Ultimate Scones (page 63), which can be topped with both the 10-minute Cheat's Lemon Curd (page 64) and this quick compote.

QUICK COMPOTE

MAKES around 175g/6oz
PREP 2 mins
COOK 4 mins

150g/5½oz frozen berries
   (I normally use blueberries
   or raspberries or a mixture)
2 tbsp granulated or caster
   sugar
grated zest of ½ lemon
   (optional)

1 Put the berries, sugar and lemon zest, if using, into a heatproof bowl and heat in a microwave oven on medium for 3–4 minutes, stirring halfway through, until the berries are soft and in a syrupy liquid.

2 Cool completely, then cover and store in the fridge for up to 3 days.

We all need a bit of sunshine in our life and the addition of pineapple and passion fruit to this bright and zingy cake makes it taste like summer! It's perfect for a summer garden party or sliced for a cute afternoon tea.

ROASTED PINEAPPLE & PASSION CAKE

SERVES 8
PREP 20 mins, plus cooling
COOK 1½ hours

400g/14oz pineapple flesh, cubed (if using fresh, remove the skin with a serrated knife, cut out the core and dice the flesh; if using canned, drain it well and dice)
200g/7oz/generous ¾ cup unsalted butter, softened, plus extra for greasing
200g/7oz/1 cup caster sugar
3 eggs
200g/7oz/1½ cups self-raising flour
1 tsp vanilla extract
2 tbsp milk

For the icing

150g/5½oz/⅔ cup unsalted butter, softened
300g/10½oz/generous 2 cups icing sugar, sifted
2 large passion fruit, sliced in half and pulp scooped out
about 1 tbsp hot water

1 Preheat the oven to 180°C/160°C fan/gas 4. Grease a 900g/2lb loaf tin (about 29 x 15.5 x 7.5cm/11½ x 6 x 3in) with a little butter and line with baking paper (or use a loaf tin liner).

2 Place your diced pineapple flesh on a flat baking sheet in a single layer and roast for 20 minutes, turning halfway through, until it starts to turn slightly golden and becomes a little drier. Transfer to a plate and leave to cool.

3 Beat together the butter and caster sugar in a large bowl or stand mixer for around 4 minutes until soft, light and fluffy. Gradually add in each egg until smooth (don't worry if it curdles at this point, it'll come together when you add the flour). Fold in the flour and vanilla until your mix is smooth, loosening it by mixing in the milk. Mix in most of the roasted pineapple chunks, saving 2 tablespoons for decoration.

4 Transfer the mixture to your lined loaf tin and level the top. Bake for 1 hour 10 minutes–1¼ hours until golden and a skewer inserted into the centre comes out clean (put some foil over the top if it's colouring too much towards the end of baking). Cool in the tin for 30 minutes, then turn out onto a wire rack to cool completely.

5 For the icing, in the bowl of a stand mixer or in a large bowl using an electric whisk, beat together the butter, icing sugar and the pulp from 1½ of the passion fruit for around 5 minutes until it's pale and fluffy, adding in enough of the hot water to loosen. You can either spread the icing over the top of your cake, or put the icing in a piping bag fitted with an open star nozzle and pipe in rows on top of the cake until it's all covered. Top with the remaining roast pineapple pieces and passion fruit pulp. Store in an airtight container for up to 4 days.

SNACKS

It's a firm belief of mine that snacking is important.
Feeling tired? Snack. Watching a film? Snack.
Putting off writing that email? Snack. Back in
school, when eating in class was forbidden, I'd be
the girl with a Gold biscuit bar in her pencil case
or Wagon Wheel up her sleeve – so this chapter is
very important to me. When you're short on cash,
don't have anything in your cupboards but need a
snack, instead of running to your local shop in your
dressing gown, why not try some of these? The Easy
Flatbreads (page 79) are my go-to as there's always
half a bag of self-raising flour knocking around, and
the remains of a yogurt that is about to turn in the
back of the fridge. If you're looking for something
to slather onto a slice of toast, the Paloma Marmalade
(page 70) is a winner as is the Any Berry Jam
(page 72), easy to make in batches and then use
at breakfast or give to friends as presents.

GF DF VG

I use jam sugar in my marmalade as an extra safety blanket, so I know that it's definitely going to set. I love marmalade, but Seville oranges can be expensive and hard to come by, so I usually make it with grapefruit. I then discovered that it's improved so much by adding tequila and salt (what isn't?!), similar to the Paloma cocktail. It makes a perfect gift, and is delicious slathered on toast as a snack.

PALOMA MARMALADE

MAKES 6 x 300-ml/
10fl-oz/1¼-cup jars
PREP 25 mins, plus setting
COOK 2 hours

2 red or pink grapefruit
    (around 600g/1lb 5oz total
    weight)
2 limes (around 200g/7oz
    total weight)
juice of 1 lemon
1.8kg/4lb/9 cups jam sugar
40ml/1½fl oz/2¾ tbsp tequila
1 tsp fine sea salt

1   Put a couple of saucers into the freezer (you will use these later to check when the marmalade is ready). Wash the grapefruit and limes and cut the ends off, then cut them into quarters, removing any seeds. Finely slice them and put into a large, deep saucepan with the juice that's released when cut, the lemon juice and 1.3 litres/2¼ pints/5½ cups of water.

2   Bring to the boil, then reduce the heat, cover and simmer for 30 minutes. Remove the lid and simmer for another 25–30 minutes until the peel has softened.

3   Tip in the sugar and stir until dissolved, bring to the boil, then reduce the heat and simmer for around 1 hour, stirring occasionally so the peel doesn't stick. To test whether it is ready, put a teaspoonful of the marmalade onto one of the chilled saucers and if it turns gelatinous, thickens and begins to set, then it's ready. If not, continue to simmer and check every 5 minutes.

4   Remove from the heat, skim any scum off the surface, then stir in the tequila and salt and leave to sit for 20 minutes to cool slightly.

5   Carefully funnel or ladle the hot marmalade into six 300-ml/10fl-oz/1¼-cup sterilized jam jars (see Tip) and seal with the lids while it's still hot. Store in a cool, dark cupboard for up to 6 months. Once opened, store in the fridge for up to 2 weeks.

TIP To sterilize your jars, preheat your oven to 140°C/120°C fan/gas 1. Wash your jars and lids, then rinse so there's no soap, but don't dry them. Lay the jars on their sides on a baking tray, not touching each other, and put in the oven for 20 minutes. Boil the lids in a saucepan of water for 20 minutes, then drain and leave to dry naturally (don't wipe them).

There are often leftover berries that are about to go off in the back of the fridge, and instead of wasting them, I tend to freeze them in a bag ready for when I have enough to make this jam! It's a great way of saving on waste and making a sweet tart jam that makes perfect gifts, too. It's great to add apples into the jam as well as they give it a bit of sweetness, and they're good to bulk it out as they're far cheaper than berries!

ANY BERRY JAM

MAKES 4 x 300-ml/
10fl-oz/1¼-cup jars
PREP 5 mins, plus setting
COOK 50 mins

600g/1lb 5oz/4 large Granny
   Smith or Bramley apples,
   peeled, cored and cut into
   2cm/¾in chunks
grated zest and juice of
   1 lemon or lime
400g/14oz any berries, frozen
   or fresh (I normally use a
   mix of frozen blackberries,
   strawberries and
   raspberries)
1kg/2lb 4oz/5 cups jam sugar

1 Put the apples into a large, deep pan along with the citrus zest and juice and 275ml/9½fl oz/scant 1¼ cups of water. Bring up to the boil and then simmer over a low-medium heat for 8 minutes until the apples are almost soft.

2 Put two saucers in your freezer (you will use these later to check when the jam is ready). Add the berries into your apple pan along with the sugar, stir so that the sugar dissolves and then bring to the boil. Turn the heat down to low and simmer for 40–45 minutes, stirring occasionally, until the jam has become thick and the fruit has broken down slightly – the apples will turn jammy and gem-like.

3 To test if the jam is ready, put a teaspoonful of the jam on one of the chilled saucers and if it turns gelatinous and thickens, wrinkling when you run your finger through it, then it's good to go! If not, simmer it for a bit longer and test again. Remove from the heat and leave it to cool and settle for 10 minutes, then skim off any scum that has risen to the surface.

4 Carefully funnel or ladle the hot jam into four 300-ml/10fl-oz/1¼-cup sterilized jam jars (see Tip on page 70) and seal with the lids while it's still hot. Store in a cool, dark cupboard for up to 6 months. Once opened, store in the fridge for up to 2 weeks.

All my Welsh friends (there are a lot of them) love bara brith, so it's now a staple in my life. Imagine a rich fruit cake that's speedy to make and tastes even better two days later, toasted and slathered in butter. This is it!

BARA BRITH

SERVES 8
PREP 15 mins, plus cooling
COOK 1½ hours

2 black or earl grey tea bags
300ml/10fl oz/1¼ cups boiling
    water
350g/12oz mixed dried fruit
    (I use a mixture of sultanas
    and mixed peel)
grated zest and juice of
    1 lemon
225g/8oz/generous 1 cup soft
    dark brown sugar
2 tsp ground mixed spice
275g/9¾oz/2 cups self-raising
    flour
2 eggs
3 tbsp runny honey

1   Put the tea bags, boiling water, dried fruit and lemon zest and juice into a saucepan and cook over a medium heat for 5 minutes, stirring until the fruit has softened. Pour the fruit and liquid into a large heatproof bowl, remove the tea bags and leave to cool for 20 minutes.

2   Preheat the oven to 160°C/140°C fan/gas 3 and line a 900g/2lb loaf tin (about 29 x 15.5 x 7.5cm/11½ x 6 x 3in) with baking paper (or use a loaf tin liner). Add the sugar, mixed spice, flour, eggs and 2 tablespoons of the honey into the fruit mix, stirring until everything has combined. Tip into the lined tin and level with the back of a spoon.

3   Bake for 1¼–1½ hours until cooked through and a skewer inserted into the centre comes out clean. Brush the remaining honey over the top of the cake to glaze and then leave it to cool completely in the tin.

4   Once cool, turn out and serve in slices slathered with butter. Keep in an airtight container (or wrapped) for up to 4 days.

DF

These bagels are so satisfying to make and are the perfect thing for piling fillings into for breakfast, plus they are so much better than shop-bought ones (not that I'm bragging).

ULTIMATE BAGELS

MAKES 8
PREP 40 mins, plus about
1 hour 20 mins proving,
plus cooling
COOK 30 mins (in batches)

500g/1lb 2oz/3½ cups strong
white bread flour, plus
extra for dusting
1 x 7g/⅛oz sachet easy-blend
dried yeast
2 tbsp caster sugar
2 tsp fine sea salt
325ml/11fl oz/generous
1¼ cups lukewarm water
1 egg, beaten, to glaze
4 tbsp Everything Seasoning
(page 76) (optional)

1   Put the flour into a large bowl or the bowl of a stand mixer fitted with a dough hook, mix the yeast and sugar into one side of the flour and mix the salt into the other side (so that the salt doesn't kill the yeast), then mix it all together. Gradually pour in enough warm water, mixing with your hands (or with a dough hook) until the dough is soft but not too sticky.

2   Knead the dough for 8 minutes in a stand mixer or for 10–12 minutes by hand until it is smooth, less sticky and springs back when you press into it. Return to the bowl (if you kneaded it by hand), cover with a clean tea towel and leave it to rise somewhere warm for an hour until doubled in size.

3   Lightly flour your work surface, then divide the dough into eight equal pieces, around 100g/3½oz each. Roll them into balls on the work surface, then place on a floured baking tray, leaving space between them (or keep them on the work surface), cover with the tea towel and leave for 20 minutes.

4   Preheat the oven to 220°C/200°C fan/gas 7 and line a large, flat baking sheet with baking paper. Bring a large pan of water to the boil and then reduce to a gentle simmer. To shape the dough balls into bagels, push one index finger through the middle of each ball to make a hole, then put your other index finger in the hole and swirl both around each other to enlarge it to a 4cm/1½in hole.

5   Working in two batches, place the bagels in the simmering water and cook for 1–2 minutes on each side until puffed up. Then fish them out with a spider strainer, drain and place them 5cm/2in apart on the lined baking sheet. Brush them with beaten egg to glaze and sprinkle over the seasoning, if you like. Bake for 22 minutes until golden brown, then remove from the oven, cover with a clean tea towel (this allows them to soften as they steam while they cool) and leave to cool completely. Serve. Keep in an airtight container for up to 3 days or freeze for up to 3 months (slice them in half before freezing, then defrost in the toaster).

My American friends always rave about 'everything seasoning' which is usually used to top bagels but can also be sprinkled as a flavour boost onto everything from salads, to flavouring butter, adding to popcorn or as a topper for soups – truly everything. I tend to make a big batch of this and store it for when I make bagels or want to pimp up a lunch.

EVERYTHING SEASONING

MAKES around 100g/3½oz
PREP 2 mins
NO COOK

3 tbsp white sesame seeds
3 tbsp black sesame seeds
3 tbsp poppy seeds
2 tsp garlic granules
2 tsp onion granules
1 tbsp sea salt flakes

1 Mix all the ingredients together in a bowl or container until combined. Store in an airtight container for up to a month.

Soda bread is one of the easiest breads to make because it doesn't need proving. The addition of sweet, sticky caramelized onions in the dough takes this to the next level.

CARAMELIZED ONION SODA BREAD

SERVES 8 (makes 1 medium loaf)
PREP 15 mins, plus cooling
COOK 1¼ hours

1 tbsp olive oil
2 onions, halved and finely sliced
2 tsp fine sea salt
1 tsp caster or granulated sugar
juice of 1 lemon
300ml/10fl oz/1¼ cups full-fat milk
450g/1lb/scant 3½ cups plain wholemeal flour, plus extra for dusting
1 tsp bicarbonate of soda

1 Put the oil into a large frying pan over a medium heat, add in the onions and fry for 10 minutes, adding a splash of water if they start to stick. Sprinkle over 1 teaspoon of the salt and the 1 teaspoon of sugar and stir through, then cook for another 10 minutes until soft and golden, making sure if you've added a splash of water that it's evaporated. Tip onto a plate and leave to cool completely. These can be made the day before and refrigerated overnight.

2 Preheat the oven to 200°C/180°C fan/gas 6. Lightly flour a flat baking sheet. Add the lemon juice into the milk and leave to curdle slightly for 2 minutes.

3 Put the flour, the remaining salt, the bicarb and cooled onions into a large bowl and mix with your fingertips until all the onions are coated in the flour. Gradually add in the milk mixture (you may not need it all), mixing it in with your hands until you have a soft but not very sticky dough. Knead gently for 2 minutes until the dough is smooth, shape into a ball and place on the floured baking sheet.

4 Dust the top with a little flour, then, using a sharp knife, score a cross on top, about 0.5cm/¼in deep. Bake for 50–55 minutes until golden brown – when you tap the bottom of the loaf it should sound hollow. Transfer to a wire rack to cool. Serve warm or cold in slices. Keep in an airtight container (or wrapped) for up to 4 days. Freeze wrapped slices for up to 2 months, then defrost overnight or in the toaster.

Are you like me and constantly craving carbs? If so, try these flatbreads. They're simple to make, using things you have in your cupboard, and they're perfect for lunch or as a snack. These flatbreads are great paired with the Roasted Carrot Hummus (page 80) or Leftover Herb Dip (page 81).

EASY FLATBREADS

MAKES 6
PREP 5 mins
COOK 10–20 mins
 (in batches)

200g/7oz/1½ cups self-raising flour, plus extra for dusting
½ tsp baking powder
a big pinch of fine sea salt
150g/5½oz/⅔ cup full-fat natural yogurt

1 Put all the ingredients into a bowl and mix with your hands until you get a smooth dough (adding a little more yogurt if you need to), then knead for 1 minute until it all comes together.

2 Dust your work surface with flour and divide the dough into six plum-sized pieces, then roll out each one into a 12cm/4½in circle.

3 Heat a large frying pan or griddle pan over a medium heat. Once hot, place one or two of the flatbreads into the pan (depending on the size of your pan) and cook for 1–2 minutes until puffed up, then flip over and cook for another 1–2 minutes. Wrap the cooked flatbreads in a clean tea towel, so they steam and become soft. Continue cooking in batches until they're all cooked. Serve warm. These will keep in an airtight container for up to 2 days, or you can freeze them individually wrapped and defrost before serving.

I'm always on the hunt to find ways to add extra vegetables into dishes. The toasty roasted carrots in this hummus add a delicious sweetness, and paired with lemon zest and paprika, create a dreamy dip. I tend to make a big batch of this at the beginning of the week, although it's easily halved if you want less.

ROASTED CARROT HUMMUS

MAKES around 1kg/2lb 4oz
PREP 10 mins
COOK 35 mins

400g/14oz carrots, peeled and chopped into 2cm/¾in chunks
1 x 400g/14oz can chickpeas, drained and rinsed
6 tbsp olive oil, plus extra to serve
2 tsp sweet smoked paprika
a big pinch of fine sea salt
4 garlic cloves, unpeeled
grated zest and juice of 1 lemon
3 tbsp tahini

1 Preheat the oven to 200°C/180°C fan/gas 6. Put the carrots on one side of a baking tray and a third of the chickpeas on the other. Drizzle with 2 tablespoons of the olive oil, then sprinkle over the paprika and salt, dividing it between the two sides. Toss each side to mix (as we will use them separately once cooked), then add the garlic cloves to the tray. Roast for 35 minutes, tossing halfway through, until softened. Allow to cool slightly for 5 minutes.

2 Squeeze the garlic out if its skin into a food processor, then add the warm cooked carrots, remaining olive oil, the lemon zest and juice and tahini. Blitz the mixture for around 5 minutes until you have a smooth mixture, then add 50ml/2fl oz/3½ tbsp of water and blitz to combine.

3 Spoon the hummus into a dish, top with a swirl of olive oil and then sprinkle over the roasted crispy chickpeas. Serve. Store in an airtight container in the fridge for up to 4 days.

Much to my flatmate's dismay, there always seem to be several packets of herbs I've bought going off in the bottom of the fridge. So, to keep the peace, I created this delicious dip, which is great for dunking bread into or even using as a sauce for cooked pasta.

LEFTOVER HERB DIP

MAKES around 250g/9oz
PREP 5 mins, plus cooling
COOK 2 mins

2 tbsp olive oil
3 garlic cloves, finely sliced
¼–½ tsp dried chilli flakes,
    plus extra to serve
4 canned (drained) anchovies
    (optional)
grated zest and juice of
    1 lemon
50g/1¾oz fresh soft green
    herbs, such as parsley,
    basil, mint, dill, coriander
100g/3½oz/scant ½ cup
    full-fat natural yogurt
25g/1oz mayonnaise
sea salt flakes and freshly
    ground black pepper

1   Put the oil, garlic, chilli flakes and anchovies, if using, into a small frying pan and sizzle over a medium heat for 1–2 minutes until it smells fragrant. Set aside to cool.

2   Put the garlic mix, lemon zest and juice and herbs along with a big pinch each of sea salt flakes and black pepper into a food processor and blitz until the herbs are finely chopped. Tip in the yogurt and mayonnaise and blitz until combined. Adjust the seasoning to taste, spoon into a dish and serve with some extra chilli flakes on top. This will keep in an airtight container in the fridge for up to 3 days.

There always seem to be leftover cherry tomatoes at the bottom of the fridge, so this is my go-to recipe to use them up. Who doesn't love basil and tomato? These make a very tempting snack-on-the-go!

TOMATO CORNBREAD MUFFINS

MAKES 10–12
PREP 15 mins, plus cooling
COOK 35 mins

225g/8oz/generous 1 cup full-fat natural yogurt
1 tbsp tomato purée
2 eggs
50ml/2fl oz/3½ tbsp olive oil
115g/4oz fine semolina
115g/4oz/generous ¾ cup plain flour
1 tbsp baking powder
½ small bunch of basil, finely chopped
200g/7oz cherry tomatoes, halved
sea salt and freshly ground black pepper

1 Preheat the oven to 190°C/170°C fan/gas 5. Put muffin cases into a 12-hole muffin tin. Put the yogurt and tomato purée into a large bowl and whisk together so the purée is evenly dispersed. Tip in the eggs and oil and whisk until combined.

2 Add the semolina, flour, baking powder, basil, a really big pinch of salt and a good crack of black pepper into the bowl and fold together with a wooden spoon until you have a smooth mixture. Fold in 150g/5½oz of the cherry tomatoes until combined.

3 Divide the mixture between the muffin cases, filling each three-quarters full. Top each with the remaining tomato halves, cut-side facing up, then crack over some black pepper. Bake for 30–35 minutes until golden brown and a skewer inserted into the centre comes out clean. Leave to cool for 5 minutes in the tin then transfer to a wire rack to cool completely before eating, otherwise they will stick to the cases. These are best eaten on the day they are made, but they will keep in an airtight container for up to 3 days.

Everyone in my flat is always after a sweet treat, so when you're in need of something sweet but don't want to go to the shop, these are perfect. I created these with ingredients I had in the kitchen – they can be whipped up in minutes and they're like a chewy cookie combined with a flapjack.

SPEEDY OAT & RAISIN COOKIES

MAKES 8
PREP 8 mins, plus cooling
COOK 13 mins

40ml/1½fl oz/2¾ tbsp vegetable or rapeseed oil
100g/3½oz/½ cup caster or granulated sugar
1 small egg
1 tsp baking powder (gluten free, if needed)
125g/4½oz/1¼ cups porridge oats (gluten free, if needed)
100g/3½oz/¾ cup raisins or sultanas

1 Preheat the oven to 200°C/180°C fan/gas 6 and line one large (or two medium) flat baking sheets with baking paper. Tip all the ingredients into a bowl and stir to combine them until you have a thick and mouldable mixture.

2 Using wetted hands (this will help as the mixture will be sticky), take a golf ball-sized piece of the mixture (about 55g/2oz), or divide the mixture into eight, then press and shape each into a ball. Place on the lined baking sheet(s), placing them 7.5cm/3in apart as they spread a lot. Press down with your palm so they're each about 1cm/½in thick and 6cm/2½in wide.

3 Bake for 12–13 minutes until golden. Leave to cool completely on the baking sheet(s). These need to cool and set completely before eating, so serve them cold. Keep in an airtight container for up to 2 days.

These light and fluffy almond and raspberry mini cakes make a lovely sweet snack to enjoy with a cup of tea. The almond extract gives a nostalgic sweet cherry-like flavour to the friands, and combined with the tart raspberries and toasty flaked almonds, makes these irresistible.

BAKEWELL FRIANDS

MAKES 12
PREP 20 mins, plus cooling
COOK 25 mins

150g/5½oz/⅔ cup unsalted butter, cubed, plus extra for greasing
45g/1½oz/⅓ cup plain flour
150g/5½oz/1 cup icing sugar, sifted, plus extra for dusting
80g/3oz/¾ cup ground almonds
1½ tsp almond extract
¼ tsp fine sea salt
4 egg whites
150g/5½oz fresh raspberries
3 tbsp flaked almonds

1 Preheat the oven to 200°C/180°C fan/gas 6 and grease a non-stick 12-hole muffin tin with butter. Melt the butter in a saucepan over a low heat for 4 minutes, stirring until it's starting to turn brown and smell nutty. Transfer into a large heatproof bowl to cool completely. Once cool, mix in the flour, icing sugar, ground almonds, almond extract and salt.

2 Whisk the egg whites in a separate bowl using an electric whisk or in a stand mixer (or by hand using a balloon whisk if you're feeling strong) until thick and frothy. Gently fold the egg whites into the flour mixture until you have a thin, frothy batter.

3 Pour the batter into your buttered moulds, filling each about three-quarters full. Put 2 large or 3 small raspberries into each mould, then sprinkle over the flaked almonds. Bake for 18–20 minutes until golden and a skewer inserted into the centre comes out clean.

4 Cool in the tin for 10 minutes, then transfer to a wire rack to cool completely (I find it easiest to remove them using a teaspoon or a blunt knife). To finish, dust a little icing sugar over the tops. Keep in an airtight container for up to 2 days.

TIP You can use the leftover egg yolks to make the Old-school Custard on page 132.

If you've never tried caramelized white chocolate before then you must try this – you'll want to keep coming back for more! It's made completely in the microwave and takes basic white chocolate up a notch by adding an intense caramel flavour just by heating it up.

CARAMELIZED WHITE CHOCOLATE & PRETZELS BARK

MAKES around 250g/9oz
PREP 2 mins, plus setting
COOK 10 mins

200g/7oz white chocolate (for the best results use good-quality chocolate, about 30% cocoa butter)
a handful of salted pretzels, crumbled
any toppings of your choice (I also like to use some sprinkles for a bit of colour)

1   Start by melting your white chocolate in a heatproof bowl in short blasts in a microwave oven on high until it's smooth and melted. To caramelize, put the white chocolate back into the microwave and heat on high for a further 5–6 minutes, giving it a stir every 20 seconds (it seems a bit tedious, but trust me, it's worth it). It'll get darker and thicker after each minute, and if it looks grainy, don't worry, just keep stirring it and it'll turn glossy – you'll end up with a deep, almost caramel-coloured chocolate that's smooth and shiny.

2   Line a flat baking sheet with a sheet of baking paper, tip the melted chocolate onto it and spread out into a rectangle roughly 30 x 20cm/ 12 x 8in. Sprinkle with the crumbled pretzels and any toppings you like – I tend to add whatever is in the cupboard, be it sprinkles, chocolate chips, freeze-dried raspberries and so on.

3   Leave to set and cool in the fridge for around 4 hours, then break off chunks (peeling off the lining paper as you go) to snack on. Store in an airtight container in the fridge for up to 4 days.

TIP If the bark looks like it has started to bloom/turn slightly white, don't worry, it's because it hasn't been tempered, but it will still taste just as good.

These are the perfect grab-and-go snack when you need some quick energy and sustenance. They're loaded with peanut butter and lots of mixed seeds to give a moreish rich texture – you'll find it hard to eat just one!

OATY PEANUT BUTTER BARS

MAKES 12
PREP 10 mins, plus 3 hours
 or overnight chilling
COOK 10 mins

125g/4½oz/generous ½ cup
 unsalted butter, cubed,
 plus extra for greasing
75g/2¾oz/⅓ cup peanut
 butter (smooth or crunchy)
40g/1½oz runny honey
50g/1¾oz/¼ cup soft dark
 brown sugar
a pinch of fine sea salt
200g/7oz/2 cups porridge
 oats (gluten free, if needed)
75g/2¾oz/¾ cup peanuts (or
 any nuts), roughly chopped
75g/2¾oz/½ cup mixed seeds
sea salt flakes, for sprinkling

1 Grease a 20cm/8in square cake tin with butter and line with baking paper. Put the butter, peanut butter, honey, sugar and salt in a saucepan over a medium heat and stir until everything has melted together. Set aside.

2 Put the oats, peanuts and seeds into a large frying pan and cook over a medium heat for 5 minutes, stirring occasionally, until lightly toasted. Tip into the melted butter mixture and stir until the oats are completely coated.

3 Tip the mixture into your prepared tin and press down with the back of a spoon to level. Sprinkle some sea salt flakes over the top, then chill in the fridge for 3 hours or overnight until set. Remove from the tin and cut into 12 bars. Store in an airtight container for up to 4 days.

GF

I usually make these sweet bites of joy around Eastertime. The marzipan in the middle combined with the almond extract in the flapjack gives these a deliciously nostalgic feel, so you'll keep coming back for more.

MARZIPAN-STUFFED FLAPJACK BITES

MAKES 16
PREP 20 mins, plus cooling
COOK 30 mins

For the flapjack

150g/5½oz/⅔ cup unsalted
  butter, cubed, plus extra
  for greasing
150g/5½oz/¾ cup soft light
  brown sugar
4 tbsp golden syrup
½ tsp fine sea salt
1 tsp almond extract
300g/10½oz/3 cups porridge
  oats (gluten free if needed)

For the filling and topping

275g/9¾oz golden marzipan
150g/3½oz dark chocolate,
  melted
2 tbsp flaked almonds,
  toasted

1 Preheat the oven to 200°C/180°C fan/gas 6. Grease a 20cm/8in loose-based square cake tin with butter and line with baking paper. Roll out the marzipan so it's 0.5cm/¼in thick and then cut it into a 20cm/8in square, using your tin as a stencil. Set aside.

2 For the flapjack, put the butter, sugar, golden syrup, salt and almond extract into a large saucepan and cook over a medium heat, stirring, until everything has melted together but is not yet boiling. Tip in the oats and stir well until coated. Put half the mixture into the bottom of the lined tin, pressing it down with the back of a spoon into an even layer.

3 Place the marzipan square on top of the flapjack base and then top with the rest of the flapjack mixture to sandwich the marzipan in the middle, pressing it down to flatten evenly and cover the marzipan. Bake for 25 minutes until golden. Leave to cool for 5 minutes, then pour over the melted chocolate, smoothing it all over the top of the flapjack. Sprinkle over the flaked almonds and leave to cool completely in the tin.

4 Once cool, remove from the tin and cut into 16 squares with a sharp knife. Keep in an airtight container for up to 4 days.

Technically soda farls are similar to soda bread or potato cakes and are normally cut into triangles, but for pure snacking purposes, these beauties are cut into small rounds so they're perfect for dunking into chutney, ketchup or garlic butter, or used as the base of canapés.

MINI SODA 'FARLS'

MAKES around 20
PREP 15 mins
COOK 16 mins (in batches)

115ml/3¾fl oz/scant ½ cup milk
juice of ½ lemon
200g/7oz/1½ cups plain flour, plus extra for dusting
½ tsp fine sea salt
1 tsp caster sugar
½ tsp bicarbonate of soda
1 tsp vegetable oil

1 Put the milk and lemon juice together in a bowl and leave to sit for 2 minutes until it starts to curdle slightly.

2 Mix the flour, salt, sugar and bicarb in a bowl. Gradually pour in the milk mixture, mixing with your hands, until you get a rough dough (you may not need all the liquid). Tip the dough out onto your floured work surface and knead for a minute until you get a smooth dough.

3 Gently roll out the dough until it's about 0.5cm/¼in thick. Cut out rounds using a 5cm/2in round cookie cutter, re-rolling until it's all used up (see Tip).

4 Heat the oil in a non-stick frying pan over a low-medium heat and fry the farls for 2 minutes on each side until golden, you may have to do this in a few batches. Transfer the cooked farls to a wire rack. Leave to cool slightly and then serve warm.

TIP To make the farls into smiley faces (which will be a hit with kids and adults alike), cut out the rounds of dough, take a straw and poke out two eyes, then use the curve of a spoon to make the mouth. Fry as above.

DF **VG**

This is a great sweet snack that can also be used as a crispy topper to decorate cakes with. The cornflake honeycomb came about after making a birthday cake for my friend Melissa who is obsessed with cornflakes, so I decided to take a cornflake cake to another level.

CORNFLAKE HONEYCOMB

MAKES around 400g/14oz
PREP 5 mins, plus cooling
COOK 15 mins

200g/7oz/1 cup caster sugar
2 tbsp golden syrup
1½ tbsp bicarbonate of soda
150g/5½oz/6 cups cornflakes
    (plain or crunchy nut ones)
1 tsp sea salt flakes
100g/3½oz dark chocolate,
    melted (optional, vegan
    and dairy free if needed)

1   Preheat the oven to 200°C/180°C fan/gas 6 and line a large, flat baking sheet with baking paper. Tip the caster sugar and golden syrup into a large, deep saucepan, then cook over a medium heat for 5–7 minutes until the mixture has fully melted and turned a deep amber colour. Tip the pan to shimmy the sugar around so it melts evenly – you can start to stir it when everything has fully melted, but not before.

2   Once you have a caramel, remove from the heat, then stir in the bicarb with a wooden spoon so it starts to foam. Tip in the cornflakes and stir so that all the cornflakes are coated, working quickly so the honeycomb doesn't set.

3   Tip the coated cornflakes out onto your lined baking sheet and roughly spread them out. Sprinkle over the sea salt flakes. Bake for 5–6 minutes until the cornflakes are golden and have become slightly more matt. Leave to cool completely on the baking sheet, then chop/ break up into bite-sized pieces.

4   If you like, you can then dunk these pieces in the melted chocolate, then leave them to set on a sheet of baking paper. Store in an airtight container for up to 3 days.

DINNER

PARTIES

Dinner parties don't have to be formal affairs, unless
you want them to be. My dinner parties tend to be
less candelabras and serviettes and more napkins and
mismatched plates in the flat. It's the perfect excuse
to bring your friends and loved ones around a table
to enjoy your food and company. Dinner parties
don't have to be stressful! A lot of these recipes
can be made in advance and simply put together
that evening, so you, even a few wines down, can
still assemble what appears to be a masterpiece of
a dessert. Try my tasty one-pot Cherry Tomato and
Blue Cheese Cobbler (page 96), then for dessert
choose a delicious bake like Brown Sugar Pavlova
(page 102) or a no-cook iced dessert such as my
No-churn Tiramisu Ice Cream Terrine (page 114).

CONFETTI & COCKTAILS

Whenever I have a few friends round, especially on a cold rainy day, a cheesy, spicy, rich tomato stew topped with fluffy, dumpling-like scones is the dish I always make. It's comforting and perfect with a few glasses of red wine.

CHERRY TOMATO & BLUE CHEESE COBBLER

SERVES 4–6
PREP 15 mins
COOK 1 hour 5 mins

For the sauce

1 tbsp vegetable or olive oil
2 onions, halved and finely sliced
3 garlic cloves, grated
½ tbsp dried chilli flakes (optional)
1 tbsp fresh thyme leaves, finely chopped
1 tbsp balsamic or red wine vinegar
1 tbsp caster sugar
1 x 400g/14oz can chopped tomatoes
250ml/9fl oz/generous 1 cup boiling water
1 vegetable stock cube
400g/14oz cherry tomatoes
100g/3½oz blue cheese
sea salt and freshly ground black pepper

For the scones

200g/7oz/1½ cups self-raising flour
1 tsp baking powder
1 tbsp fresh thyme leaves, finely chopped
50g/1¾oz/½ cup Cheddar cheese, coarsely grated
a pinch of fine sea salt
100g/3½oz/scant ½ cup unsalted butter, cold and cubed
1 egg, beaten

1 For the sauce, put the oil into a shallow casserole dish that can go on the hob (see Tip) and put it over a medium heat. Add in the onions and cook for 8–10 minutes until starting to soften – you can add a splash of water if they start to stick. Add the garlic and cook for 1 minute. Tip in the chilli flakes, thyme, vinegar, sugar, canned tomatoes and boiling water, then crumble in the stock cube. Simmer for 10–15 minutes until the sauce starts to thicken.

2 Stir in the cherry tomatoes, cover and cook for 10 minutes until just starting to soften. Remove the lid, crumble in the blue cheese and stir to incorporate, then season with a little salt and a good crack of black pepper and set aside.

3 Preheat the oven to 200°C/180°C fan/gas 6. To make the scones, add the flour, baking powder, thyme, Cheddar, salt and a crack of black pepper into a large bowl and mix. Rub in the butter using your fingertips until you have a sandy consistency. Add in up to 3 tablespoons of water, mixing and squeezing with your hands until a dough forms.

4 Divide the dough into six even portions and shape each into a ball. Press the balls down slightly so they're around 2cm/¾in thick and brush with beaten egg. Place on top of the tomato stew and then bake for 35–40 minutes until the scones are golden and the stew is bubbling. Serve hot. Cool and store any leftovers in an airtight container in the fridge for up to 3 days, then serve cold or reheat until hot through.

TIP If you don't have a shallow casserole dish that can go on the hob, make the sauce in a saucepan, then pour it into a baking dish, put the scones on top and bake.

I used Stilton here, but you can use your favourite blue cheese.

DINNER PARTIES

There's something about the cheesy, salty chilli topping that makes this focaccia so incredibly hard to resist! This makes the perfect addition to any dinner party.

CHEESE, CHIVE & CHILLI FOCACCIA

SERVES 10–12
PREP 25 mins, plus
2–2½ hours proving
COOK 22 mins

500g/1lb 2oz/3½ cups strong white bread flour, plus extra for dusting
1 x 7g/⅛oz sachet easy-blend dried yeast
1 tsp caster sugar
1 tsp fine sea salt
5 spring onions, finely sliced
½ small bunch of chives, finely sliced
50g/1¾oz/½ cup Cheddar cheese, finely grated
3 tbsp olive oil, plus extra for greasing and to serve
350–375ml/12–13fl oz/ 1½–1⅔ cups lukewarm water

For the topping

50g/1¾oz/½ cup Cheddar cheese, coarsely grated
1–2 tsp dried chilli flakes (optional)
1½ tbsp olive oil
1 tsp sea salt flakes

1 Put the flour into a mixing bowl (or in the bowl of your stand mixer). Mix the yeast and sugar into one side of the flour, and the salt into the other side, then mix everything together (this stops the salt from killing the yeast).

2 Mix the spring onions, chives and Cheddar into your flour, add the olive oil, then gradually add lukewarm water, mixing until you have a slightly sticky dough (you may not need all the water). You can either combine it by hand or use the dough hook on your mixer. If you do it by hand, sprinkle the work surface with flour and tip the dough onto it, scraping around the sides of the bowl, then knead for 5–10 minutes (by hand, or in your mixer) until your dough is soft and less sticky. Put the dough into a clean bowl, cover with a clean tea towel and leave to prove in a warm place for 1–1½ hours until doubled in size.

3 Heavily oil a 20 x 30cm/8 x 12in deep baking tin (if you find your tin is quite old and tends to stick, line it with baking paper, too). Tip the dough into the tin, then stretch it to fill the tin. Cover with a tea towel and leave to prove for another hour until doubled in size.

4 Preheat the oven to 220°C/200°C fan/gas 7. Press your fingers into the dough to make dimples all over (oiling your hands makes it easier to do this as they won't stick to the dough). For the topping, sprinkle the Cheddar and chilli flakes (if using) evenly over the dough. Mix the olive oil with 1 tablespoon of cold water and drizzle over the bread, then sprinkle over the sea salt flakes to finish.

5 Bake for 20–22 minutes until golden. Remove from the oven, cover the focaccia with a clean tea towel and leave to cool. Cut into squares and serve warm or cold with extra olive oil on the side. Keep in an airtight container for up to 4 days.

DF **VG**

These beautiful, golden, fluffy twisted bread rolls are the perfect gift to bring to a dinner party (flowers and chocolates are overdone). They're the ideal way to start a meal, slathered in butter (or vegan/dairy-free butter) and sprinkled with sea salt flakes.

TWISTED BREAD ROLLS

MAKES 10
PREP 30 mins, plus 1½ hours proving
COOK 22 mins

400g/14oz/2¾ cups strong white bread flour
1 x 7g/⅛oz sachet easy-blend dried yeast
1 tsp caster sugar
1 tsp fine sea salt
3 tbsp olive oil
250ml/9fl oz/generous 1 cup lukewarm water
1 egg, beaten (or use 2 tbsp plant-based milk, if vegan)
2 tbsp nigella seeds (optional)

1 Put the flour into a large mixing bowl or the bowl of a stand mixer. Mix the yeast and sugar into one side of the flour and the salt into the other side, then mix everything together (this stops the salt from killing the yeast).

2 Pour in the oil and then gradually add in the warm water (you may not need it all) until you have a soft dough. Knead either by hand or using a dough hook in a stand mixer for 8–10 minutes until you have a smooth dough that isn't sticky. Place into a clean bowl, cover and leave in a warm place for an hour until doubled in size.

3 Line two large, flat baking sheets with baking paper. Divide the dough into 10 even portions. For each roll, split each piece of dough in half and roll each half into a 25cm/10in sausage/log. Squeeze two ends together, then twist both pieces around each other into a spiral. Shape the spiral into a circle by wrapping it around itself like a snail and pinching the end in so it keeps the shape. Shape the remaining portions of dough in the same way, placing each one on a lined baking sheet as you go, spacing the rolls about 8cm/3¼in apart. Cover and leave to prove for 30 minutes.

4 Preheat the oven to 200°C/180°C fan/gas 6. Brush all the rolls with the beaten egg (or milk) and sprinkle over the nigella seeds, if you like. Bake for 18–22 minutes until golden brown and when you tap the bottom of a roll it sounds hollow. Transfer to a wire rack to cool, and serve warm or cold. Keep in an airtight container for up to 4 days.

When I was training to be a pastry chef, we were taught how to make a classic tarte tatin. These days, several wines down at a dinner party, the last thing I want to be doing is making caramel, which is how these easy but impressive tartelettes came about. You don't have to make a caramel, they can be whipped up quickly and are perfect served with ice cream or custard.

CHEAT'S APPLE TARTELETTES

SERVES 4
PREP 10 mins
COOK 30 mins

4 tsp runny honey or maple
    syrup
1 large red-skinned eating
    apple, quartered,
    cored and finely sliced
    lengthways
1 tbsp soft dark brown sugar
    or ½ tbsp caster sugar
1 tsp ground cinnamon
1 x 320g/11½oz ready-rolled
    shortcrust pastry sheet
1 tbsp icing sugar
vanilla ice cream or warm
    custard, to serve

1   Preheat the oven to 200°C/180°C fan/gas 6 and line a large, flat baking sheet with a sheet of baking paper. On one part of the lined baking sheet, drizzle 1 teaspoon of honey or maple syrup in a circular motion so it fills around a 8–9 cm/3¼–3½in circle. Continue in the same way until you have four circles of drizzled honey, each placed a little apart on the baking sheet.

2   Toss the apple slices, brown or caster sugar and cinnamon together in a bowl. Arrange some apple slices, slightly overlapping, in a circle on top of each honey circle.

3   Unroll the shortcrust pastry sheet and cut it into four equal rectangles, trimming off the corners of each to make an oval (that will cover the apple slices). Place each pastry oval over the apple slices, then push and crimp around the edges to form a circle of pastry covering the apples. Prick the top of the pastry all over with a fork to let the steam out. Bake for 25–30 minutes until the apple is cooked through and the pastry is golden (don't worry if some of the honey runs out).

4   Flip the apple tartelettes over with a spatula to serve and dust each with a little icing sugar to glaze. Scoop on some melty vanilla ice cream or warm custard, if you like, and eat right away. Or, cool and store in an airtight container in the fridge for up to 2 days, then reheat until hot through.

Use this as the base for other pavlovas and change up the flavours on top as you please. I love to add the Sticky Ginger Poached Pears (page 104) on top, as they add a little kick of sweet ginger, along with some toasted pecans or walnuts and a bit of mint. The brown sugar adds a toasty caramel flavour to the meringue and cream and steps up your pavlova game.

BROWN SUGAR PAVLOVA

SERVES 8
PREP 35 mins, plus cooling
COOK 1½ hours

For the pavlova
100g/3½oz/½ cup soft light brown sugar
150g/5½oz/¾ cup caster sugar
6 egg whites
3 tsp cornflour
2 tsp white wine vinegar
1 tsp vanilla paste

For the cream
300ml/10fl oz/1¼ cups double cream
2 tbsp soft light brown sugar

To serve (optional)
fruit, such as fresh berries or Sticky Ginger Poached Pears (page 104)
toasted nuts, such as pecans or walnuts
fresh mint sprigs

1   Preheat the oven to 150°C/130°C fan/gas 2. Line a large, flat baking sheet with baking paper and draw a 23–24cm/9–9½in circle on it (you can draw around a plate or cake tin to make this easier). Flip the baking paper over so that the mark is on the underside.

2   Make the pavlova. Mix together both sugars. Whisk the egg whites in a large bowl with an electric whisk or in a stand mixer for 1 minute on a medium speed until foamy. Gradually add the mixed sugars, 1 tablespoon at a time, waiting until it's combined before you add in the next one. Once all the sugar has been added, turn the speed up and then whisk for around 7 minutes until you have a thick, glossy meringue that shouldn't feel grainy when you rub a little mix between your fingers. If it does, keep whisking.

3   Fold the cornflour, vinegar and vanilla into the meringue. Dollop the meringue onto the baking paper circle and spread around to fill the drawn circle, like an igloo. Smooth the top and sides with a small palette knife or butter knife and create a little dip in the middle – you can drag the knife upwards on the sides to create a pattern.

4   Bake for 1½ hours until coloured and crisp. Turn the oven off and leave the meringue in the oven (with the door ajar) to cool completely – don't worry if it cracks slightly.

5   Once cool, make the cream. Whip the cream and sugar together in a bowl until you have soft peaks and it just holds its shape. Put the pavlova base onto a plate or platter and spoon the cream over the top, then top with your choice of fruit, toasted nuts and/or a few mint sprigs. Slice and serve. Store in an airtight container (or covered) in the fridge for up to a day.

TIPS Secure your baking paper to the baking sheet with little dots of the meringue under each corner.

You can make and bake the pavlova base 2–3 days ahead and keep it in an airtight container. The sweetened cream can be whipped ahead on the day and refrigerated until needed.

These poached pears are delicious served on top of the Brown Sugar Pavlova on page 102, sprinkled with some toasted nuts and a few sprigs of mint. They also work beautifully for breakfast with porridge, or for dessert served with ice cream and some ginger biscuits crumbled over the top.

STICKY GINGER POACHED PEARS

SERVES 4 (or serves 8 if added to a pudding)
PREP 5 mins
COOK 30 mins

300g/10½oz/1½ cups granulated or caster sugar
300g/10½oz/1½ cups soft light brown sugar
600ml/1 pint/2½ cups hot water
100g/3½oz fresh ginger, peeled and finely sliced
grated zest and juice of 1 lemon
4 ripe pears

1 Put both sugars, the hot water, ginger and lemon zest and juice into a saucepan over a medium heat and bring to the boil. While you're waiting, prepare the pears – peel them, slice in half lengthways and scoop out the tough middle part with a spoon.

2 Drop the pears into the sugary water, reduce the heat to simmering, then cut out a circle of baking paper and place it directly on top of the pears (this is called a cartouche), so the pears cook evenly and the liquid doesn't evaporate too quickly.

3 Simmer for 15 minutes, then remove the cartouche, flip the pears over, replace the cartouche and simmer for a further 10 minutes until the pears are soft and you can easily slide a knife through them. Turn the heat off and let the pears sit in the syrup (leave the cartouche in place until serving). Serve warm or cold (see the recipe intro for some other delicious ways to serve them).

4 You can make this recipe up to 2 days in advance and keep the pears covered in the syrup in an airtight container in the fridge, as this really enhances the flavour.

TIP You can save the syrup from the pears in an airtight container in the fridge for up to 1 week. It's great to drizzle on porridge, shake in a cocktail, or use for poaching more fruit.

Are you also a custard fiend? I always have a can of it in the cupboard just for custard-related emergencies or when I'm feeling nostalgic (we'll pretend I don't sit there eating it cold with a spoon). This super-quick rhubarb and custard galette is made using a really quick pastry with canned custard and rhubarb to finish. It will fast become a favourite, plus you can make it the day before!

RHUBARB & CUSTARD GALETTE

SERVES 8
PREP 25 mins
COOK 50 mins

For the dough

250g/9oz/scant 2 cups plain flour
a pinch of fine sea salt
175g/6oz/¾ cup unsalted butter, cold and cubed
50g/1¾oz/¼ cup caster sugar

For the topping

125g/4½oz canned custard
375g/13oz fresh rhubarb, cut into 5cm/2in strips (slicing any thick pieces in half lengthways)
grated zest of 1 large orange or lemon
2 tbsp caster or granulated sugar
1 tbsp milk
2 tbsp demerara sugar
maple syrup (optional)

1 Preheat the oven to 220°C/200°C fan/gas 7 and place a large, flat baking sheet in the oven to heat up (this will prevent the galette having a soggy bottom). Put all the ingredients for the dough into a large bowl and rub in the butter with your fingertips until fine breadcrumbs form. Gradually add in about 80ml/2½fl oz/5 tbsp of water, a little at a time (you may not need it all) until you have a smooth dough.

2 Roll the dough into a ball and place it between two sheets of baking paper. Roll into roughly a 31cm/12½in circle, then remove the top layer of baking paper. For the topping, spread the custard evenly over the pastry circle, leaving a 2.5cm/1in border.

3 Toss the rhubarb with the citrus zest and white sugar, then arrange on top of the custard. Fold the pastry edges up and over the rhubarb, folding over about 4cm/1½in all the way round (the fruit in the centre will not be covered with pastry).

4 Brush the pastry edges with milk and sprinkle with the demerara sugar. Slide the galette (still on the baking paper) onto the hot baking sheet in the oven and bake for 15 minutes. Turn the oven down to 190°C/170°C fan/gas 5 and bake for a further for 30–35 minutes until the pastry is deep golden and the rhubarb is soft. If you have some maple syrup, you can brush a little on top to glaze just before serving, if you like. Serve warm or cold in slices.

A neat slice of custard tart is a beautiful, elegant thing and the perfect way to end a dinner party alongside a coffee. So why not combine the two? This impressive espresso custard tart has a kick of coffee in a creamy rich filling encased in flaky pastry, and it can be made ahead.

ESPRESSO CUSTARD TART

SERVES 8–10
PREP 30 mins, plus chilling and cooling
COOK 1 hour 10 mins

For the pastry

250g/9oz/scant 2 cups plain flour, plus extra for dusting
50g/1¾oz/¼ cup caster sugar
150g/5½oz/⅔ cup unsalted butter, cold and cubed
a pinch of fine sea salt

For the filling

300ml/10fl oz/1¼ cups double cream
200ml/7fl oz/generous ¾ cup full-fat milk
1 tsp vanilla paste or vanilla extract (paste is better)
8 egg yolks
2 tbsp espresso powder
50g/1¾oz/¼ cup soft dark brown sugar
50g/1¾oz/¼ cup caster sugar
1 tbsp icing sugar, to serve (optional)

1 Start by making the pastry. Put the flour, sugar, butter and salt into a large bowl or food processor. You can either rub the butter into the flour using your fingertips until a sandy texture forms or pulse it in a food processor until it's sandy. Add in around 3 tablespoons of water until you have a soft dough that isn't too sticky.

2 Flour your work surface and roll out the dough into a circle about 0.5cm/¼in thick and big enough to line a 20cm/8in loose-based round or fluted tart tin around 3.5cm/1½in deep. Wrap the pastry around your rolling pin and drape it over the tart tin. Press into the tin, making sure to press it into the corners, then cut off any excess at the top so there's about a 2cm/¾in overhang. This pastry is very forgiving so you can patch it up if it breaks. Poke the pastry base all over with a fork. Chill in the fridge for 45 minutes until firm.

3 Preheat the oven to 180°C/160°C fan/gas 4. Scrunch up (to make it more pliable) a square piece of baking paper big enough to cover the tart tin, then open it out and place it flat in the pastry case. Fill with baking beans (or a mix of raw rice and dried beans) and bake for 15 minutes. Remove the baking beans and paper and bake for another 10 minutes until starting to turn golden brown. Leave to cool, then trim the edges with a small, sharp knife to neaten them.

continues...

4 Turn your oven down to 150°C/130°C fan/gas 2. To make the filling, put the cream, milk and vanilla into a saucepan over a medium heat and stir occasionally until it starts to simmer. Meanwhile, put the egg yolks, espresso powder and both sugars into a large, heatproof bowl and whisk by hand for a minute to combine. Gradually stream your hot milk into the egg mixture, whisking constantly, until smooth. Leave to settle for a few minutes and then skim off most of the foam (don't worry about getting it all, we'll cover the top at the end).

5 Put your tart tin onto a baking tray (this will catch any spills). Pour the custard into the pastry case right up to the top, then bake for 30–35 minutes until the edges have set and the middle has a slight wobble. Leave to cool for 10 minutes, then remove from the tin. Dust with icing sugar and either serve slightly warm at room temperature or chilled. Store in an airtight container (or covered) in the fridge for up to 2 days.

TIP I've found that brewed coffee doesn't give you as strong a flavour, but if that's all you have then you can substitute 100ml/3½fl oz/generous ⅓ cup of the milk for the same quantity of strong brewed espresso.

With an oaty, buttery peanut base, topped with a creamy layer of peanut butter ganache and a salted dark chocolate filling, this tart is a dream! Don't tell anyone but I may have had it for breakfast on a few occasions.

NO-BAKE PEANUT BUTTER CHOCOLATE TART

SERVES 10
PREP 50 mins, plus setting and 4 hours or overnight chilling
NO COOK

For the base

200g/7oz oaty biscuits (I use Hobnobs) or digestives
100g/3½oz/¾ cup salted roasted peanuts, plus extra to serve
115g/4oz/½ cup unsalted butter, melted, plus extra for greasing

For the peanut butter ganache

125g/4½oz/generous ½ cup peanut butter (smooth or crunchy, I use Manilife deep roast crunchy peanut butter), plus extra to serve
125g/4½oz/generous ½ cup double cream
100g/3½oz white chocolate, roughly chopped
50ml/2fl oz/3½ tbsp boiling water

For the chocolate filling

150g/5½oz dark chocolate, roughly chopped, plus extra to serve
215g/7½oz/1 cup double cream
150g/5½oz/¾ cup soft light brown sugar
a pinch of sea salt flakes

1 Grease just the base of a 23cm/9in loose-based round tart tin (around 4cm/1½in deep) and line with a circle of baking paper.

2 Make the base. In a food processor, blitz the biscuits and salted peanuts together until you have a sandy consistency (being careful not to over-blitz or it will turn into a paste), or place in a ziplock bag and bash with a rolling pin. Transfer to a bowl and mix in the melted butter, then tip into the prepared tin and use the back of a spoon to press the biscuit mixture over the base and up the sides of the tin. Refrigerate to set.

3 Meanwhile, make the peanut butter ganache. Put the peanut butter, double cream and white chocolate into a heatproof mixing bowl, place it over a pan of simmering water (make sure the bowl doesn't touch the water) and heat together until melted. Don't worry, it may split because of the fat content, but like magic, once melted, quickly whisk in the boiling water and you will have a thick, glossy mixture (if yours doesn't split, add the water anyway to improve the texture when it's set). Pour into the cooled biscuit base and refrigerate for 1–2 hours or until set.

4 Once set, make the chocolate filling. Place all the ingredients into a heatproof mixing bowl, place the bowl over a pan of simmering water (as before) and heat until melted and glossy, stirring occasionally. Leave to cool to room temperature, then pour on top of the peanut butter layer and leave to set in the fridge for 4 hours or overnight.

5 Carefully remove the tart from the tin – either leave it at room temperature for an hour or so to warm up slightly or lightly run a blow torch around the sides to loosen it enough. Place on a serving board, then sprinkle the top with some roughly chopped salted peanuts, a grating of dark chocolate and a drizzle of peanut butter. Serve in slices. Keep in an airtight container in the fridge for up to 3 days.

This flapjack brownie tart is deliciously buttery, sweet, salty and toasty. The brown butter flapjack case is filled with a rich chocolate brownie filling and topped with flaky sea salt. It's one of my all-time favourite recipes.

SALTED FLAPJACK BROWNIE TART

SERVES 8–10
PREP 35 mins, plus cooling and (optional) overnight chilling
COOK 40 mins

For the flapjack

100g/3½oz/scant ½ cup salted butter
100g/3½oz/½ cup soft dark brown sugar
25g/1oz golden syrup
200g/7oz/2 cups porridge oats

For the brownie

90g/3¼oz/generous ⅓ cup salted butter, cubed
90g/3¼oz dark chocolate, roughly chopped
2 eggs
150g/5½oz/¾ cup caster sugar
40g/1½oz/generous ¼ cup plain flour
25g/1oz/¼ cup unsweetened cocoa powder
50g/1¾oz white chocolate, chopped into chunks
1 tsp sea salt flakes

1   Preheat the oven to 180°C/160°C fan/gas 4. Line the base of an 18cm/7in loose-based round cake tin, around 3.5cm/1½in deep, with baking paper. (If you don't have a loose-based tin, place two long strips of parchment going across the tin, crossing over on either side so the tart is easier to lift out of the tin.) For the flapjack, melt the butter, brown sugar and golden syrup in a saucepan over a low heat, then pour in the oats and mix until combined. Tip into the lined tin and, using the back of a spoon, push the flapjack mixture over the base and up the sides of the tin until evenly spread (if it's sticking to the spoon, dampen the spoon). Bake for 10 minutes until golden, then leave to cool until needed.

2   Meanwhile, make the brownie. Melt the butter and dark chocolate together, either in a heatproof bowl in a microwave oven on medium in 20-second bursts for about 1½ minutes, stirring after every burst until melted, or place the bowl over a small pan of simmering water (make sure the bowl doesn't touch the water) and stir until melted. Set aside to cool slightly.

3   Put the eggs and caster sugar into a separate bowl and whisk together in a stand mixer or using an electric whisk (or with a whisk, by hand using some muscle) for 5 minutes or until the mixture is thick, pale and has doubled in size.

4   Gently fold the cooled melted chocolate mix into the egg mixture until combined. Fold in the flour, cocoa powder and white chocolate chunks until combined. Pour into your flapjack case, sprinkle with the sea salt flakes, then bake for 22–28 minutes or until it has a little wobble in the centre but is set around the edges. Cool completely in the tin. Once cool, you can refrigerate it overnight to make perfect slices, if you like. Serve in slices. Keep in an airtight container in the fridge for up to 4 days.

TIP If you've left the tart in the fridge overnight, you can either leave it out at room temperature for an hour or loosen around the edge with a blow torch to help remove it from the tin.

This is two of the best desserts in one – a tiramisu mixed with a Viennetta-style ice cream – and to top it off it's no-churn, which means you don't need an ice-cream maker nor have to make a custard! It's perfect for dinner parties as you can make it well in advance.

NO-CHURN TIRAMISU ICE CREAM TERRINE

SERVES 8–10
PREP 20 mins, plus overnight freezing
NO COOK

1½ tbsp coffee granules dissolved in 60ml/ 2¼fl oz/4 tbsp boiling water, or 60ml/2¼fl oz/ 4 tbsp brewed espresso coffee
75ml/2½fl oz/5 tbsp Marsala or coffee liqueur
8–10 savoiardi or sponge fingers
1 tbsp vanilla paste
100g/3½oz/scant ½ cup mascarpone cheese
300ml/10fl oz/1¼ cups double cream
275g/9¾oz condensed milk
200g/7oz dark chocolate, melted and cooled slightly
1 tbsp unsweetened cocoa powder

1   In a small bowl, mix together the coffee and Marsala or coffee liqueur. Line a 900g/2lb loaf tin (about 29 x 15.5 x 7.5cm/11½ x 6 x 3in) either with two strips of baking paper or with clingfilm (splashing the tin with a little water first so it sticks to the sides) overhanging the sides. Cut the sponge fingers so they fit widthways across the tin, dunk each one into the warm coffee mixture for 10 seconds on each side, then line them up over the base of the tin.

2   Put the remaining coffee mixture into a large bowl and cool, then add in the vanilla, mascarpone, cream and condensed milk and whisk using an electric whisk for around 5 minutes until it thickens and soft peaks form.

3   Spoon a third of the cream mixture on top of the sponge fingers, tapping the tin down so the mixture goes into the gaps between them. Drizzle over half the melted chocolate and spread it out so all the cream is covered. Pour over another third of the cream mixture and spread it out. Top with the remaining melted chocolate, spreading it as before, then top with the remaining cream and spread in an even layer.

4   Put the overhanging baking paper or clingfilm over the top to seal it and then put it level in the freezer overnight. Once frozen, wrap it tightly and freeze for up to 2 months if you're not serving it just yet. When you want to serve, leave the terrine at room temperature for 10 minutes and then tip it upside down onto a plate, remove the tin and peel off the baking paper or clingfilm. Dust with the cocoa powder, slice and serve. To slice perfect portions, dunk your sharp knife into a jug of boiling water, then wipe dry and slice.

This technique is amazing for making crème brûlée as you don't need to spend hours cooking it in a water bath. I learnt it from Andy Ditchfield and the amazing pastry team at the House of Commons. It's been a game changer and is so much easier than the traditional method.

ORANGE & CARDAMOM CRÈME BRÛLÉE

SERVES 6
PREP 20 mins, plus 1 hour infusion and 6 hours or overnight setting
COOK 10 mins

600ml/1 pint/2½ cups double cream
grated or pared zest of 2 large oranges
1 tbsp green cardamom pods, crushed
100g/3½oz/½ cup caster sugar
4 egg yolks
1 tsp vanilla paste
6 tbsp demerara sugar

1 Tip the double cream into a saucepan along with the orange zest and cardamom pods and place over a medium heat until it starts to boil. Take off the heat, then cover and leave to infuse for 1 hour, or if you want to get a stronger flavour, you can leave it in the fridge overnight.

2 Strain the cream into a larger saucepan and place over a medium heat until it starts to boil. Meanwhile, put the caster sugar, egg yolks and vanilla into a heatproof bowl and whisk for a few minutes until starting to become pale.

3 Pour a quarter of the hot cream on top of the egg yolks and whisk to combine. Turn the heat down to low-medium and then tip the egg yolk mixture back into the cream pan, whisking as you add it. Continue to whisk the mix for around 3–4 minutes until it starts to thicken (technically it should be around 82°C and it will be just when it's about to start simmering). The custard should coat the back of a spoon, and when you run your finger through it you should see a line on the spoon.

4 Take off the heat and pass it through a sieve into a jug. Divide the thick custard between six 125ml/4fl oz/½ cup heatproof ramekins or mugs, cool, then refrigerate for 6 hours or overnight until set.

5 When you're ready to serve, sprinkle a tablespoonful of the demerara sugar onto the top of each brûlée in a thin layer, then either blow torch the tops so you get a crisp even caramel, or put under a preheated hot grill and keep the dishes/mugs moving around so the sugar caramelizes evenly. Cool for a couple of minutes until firm, then serve. Cover and store the custards in the fridge without the caramelized topping, for up to 3 days, then sprinkle with sugar and caramelize when you want to eat them.

TIP You can make the dish using one cinnamon stick instead of the cardamom, if you'd prefer.

GF

The tactic for this recipe came to me when I had no room in the freezer for ice, and a load of ice cream (priorities) and I desperately wanted an espresso martini (again, priorities). So I packed some vanilla ice cream into a cocktail shaker to chill it. It's perfect as you don't need to make a sugar syrup to sweeten it!

ESPRESSO MARTINI AFFOGATO

MAKES 2
PREP 5 mins
NO COOK

100ml/3½fl oz/generous
⅓ cup vodka
50ml/2fl oz/3½ tbsp espresso
50ml/2fl oz/3½ tbsp coffee
liqueur
50g/1¾oz vanilla or coffee ice
cream, plus 2 extra scoops
to serve
ice, to serve
unsweetened cocoa powder,
to finish

1 Fill two glasses with ice. Place all the ingredients, except the cocoa powder, into a cocktail shaker and shake with some force (to get it frothy and so the ice cream melts). Strain into your ice-filled glasses.

2 Top each portion with a scoop of ice cream and finish with a dusting of cocoa powder. Serve immediately.

Want to make a dessert that looks fancy enough for a dinner party, but is actually deceptively simple and can be prepared in advance? These delicate mille-feuille are your answer. You can bake the crispy pastry a few days before, then whip up the cream and assemble them in a flash when you're ready for dessert.

PISTACHIO & RASPBERRY MILLE-FEUILLE

MAKES 6
PREP 30 mins, plus cooling
COOK 30 mins

1 x 375g/13oz ready-rolled puff pastry sheet
200ml/7fl oz/generous ¾ cup double cream
3 tbsp caster sugar
200g/7oz fresh raspberries, halved
2 tbsp shelled pistachios, toasted and roughly chopped
24 whole fresh raspberries
50g/1¾oz shelled pistachios, finely chopped (or use pistachio nibs)

1 Preheat the oven to 200°C/180°C fan/gas 6 and line a large, flat baking sheet with baking paper. Unroll the pastry onto the baking paper. Place another heavy baking sheet on top so the pastry is sandwiched between the two sheets (or if your baking sheet isn't heavy, you can put something like an empty baking dish on top of it) and bake for 25–30 minutes until it's turning golden and crisp.

2 Remove from the oven, take the top baking sheet off and let the pastry cool completely. Using a sharp knife, straighten the edges and cut off any excess, then cut the pastry into 8 x 5cm/3¼ x 2in rectangles. I get around 21, which is three more than needed, but it's good to have some spare.

3 Whip the cream and sugar together in a large bowl using an electric whisk or in a stand mixer until it thickens to soft peaks and holds its shape. Spoon into a piping bag and cut off the end to create a medium-sized hole.

4 To assemble each mille-feuille (assemble them all at the same time), place one pastry rectangle on a chopping board and pipe 4 blobs of cream diagonally onto it, alternating each blob with a raspberry half, then sprinkle some toasted pistachios on top of the cream. Put another pastry rectangle on top and repeat with 4 more blobs of cream, raspberry halves and toasted pistachios. Put a final pastry rectangle on top, then pipe on 4 blobs of cream, alternating with 4 whole raspberries this time. Sprinkle with some finely chopped pistachios (or nibs) to finish. Serve right away (these will keep wrapped or in an airtight container in the fridge for up to a day, but they are best served immediately).

TIP I find it easier to match up the baked pastry rectangles into groups of three, so that each mille-feuille has the same size layers.
If the raspberries are small, you can use them whole rather than cut in half.

COMFORT

FOOD

Have you ever had one of those days where you just *need* a slice of cake, or a friend has come for dinner in need of cheering up? These recipes are for those moments. Filled with nostalgic joy, from a Lighter Jam Roly-poly with Old-school Custard (pages 135 and 132) to Seaside Ring Doughnuts (page 140) just like the ones you used buy in a paper bag at the beach – these are aimed at putting a smile on your face. A personal favourite in this chapter are the Hungover Sausage Sarnie Pasties (page 125) as they serve as an ultimate pick-me-up the morning after a late night. Filled with comforting caramelized onions and tomatoes, they're the thing I grab from the freezer when all I want to do is have a pity party and lay in bed watching *Gilmore Girls*.

SOUL FOOD

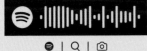

Sometimes, all you need is a load of filthy cheese and carbs to improve your day, which is how this breakfast bake was invented. I like to add a little bit of cayenne, Worcestershire sauce and a sprinkle of dried chilli flakes to give it a little kick.

TRIPLE CHEESE FRENCH TOAST BAKE

SERVES 6
PREP 20 mins
COOK 30 mins

3 eggs
200ml/7fl oz/generous ¾ cup milk
1 tsp fine sea salt
2 tsp Worcestershire sauce
a pinch of cayenne pepper
150g/5½oz/⅔ cup cream cheese
6–8 thick slices of bread
150g/5½oz/1½ cups Cheddar cheese, grated
50g/1¾oz/½ cup porridge oats
2 tbsp finely grated Parmesan cheese
1 tbsp olive or vegetable oil, plus extra for greasing
1½ tsp dried chilli flakes
freshly ground black pepper

1 Preheat the oven to 190°C/170°C fan/gas 5. Grease a 20 x 30cm/8 x 12in deep baking dish with oil. Put the eggs, milk, salt, a big crack of black pepper, the Worcestershire sauce and cayenne into a medium bowl and whisk together.

2 Spread the cream cheese over the slices of bread (on one side only). Dunk each slice into the egg mixture, making sure each side is covered, then place into the prepared baking dish, slightly overlapping each slice. Pour over the remaining egg mix, then sprinkle over half the Cheddar.

3 Put the oats, Parmesan, remaining Cheddar, the olive or vegetable oil and ½ teaspoon of the chilli flakes into a bowl and toss together with your hands so everything is combined and coated in the oil. Evenly spread this mix over the top of the bread slices.

4 Bake for 30 minutes or until the egg custard is set and the top is golden brown and crisp. Sprinkle with the remaining chilli flakes and serve warm. Store any leftovers in an airtight container in the fridge for up to 2 days – eat cold or reheat (in an ovenproof dish) in a preheated oven at 200°C/180°C fan/gas 6 for 20 minutes.

I wanted to make something you could quickly take from the freezer (see Tip) when tired and/or hungover, and shove in the oven for a deeply satisfying breakfast – these hit the spot!

HUNGOVER SAUSAGE SARNIE PASTIES

MAKES 4
PREP 40 mins, plus chilling
COOK 55 mins

For the filling

1 tbsp oil from the sun-dried
    tomatoes (see below)
2 onions, halved and finely
    sliced
a pinch of fine sea salt
4 pork sausages (around
    250g/9oz total weight)
2 garlic cloves, crushed
75g/2¾oz sun-dried tomatoes
    in oil, drained and finely
    chopped
4–5 tbsp tomato ketchup
sea salt and freshly ground
    black pepper

For the pastry

425g/15oz/3¼ cups plain flour,
    plus extra for dusting
215g/7½oz/scant 1 cup
    unsalted butter, cold and
    cubed
1 tsp fine sea salt
1 egg, beaten

1   For the filling, heat the oil in a frying pan over a medium heat, add in the onions and salt and fry for 8–10 minutes until starting to soften. Squeeze chunks of sausage meat out of the skins into the pan and fry over a high heat for 3 minutes until starting to brown (they don't need to be cooked through), breaking them up with your wooden spoon. Tip in the garlic and sun-dried tomatoes, season with salt and pepper and fry for a minute. Take off the heat and stir in the ketchup, then tip into a bowl and leave to cool completely.

2   Meanwhile, for the pastry, put the flour, butter and salt into a bowl and rub the butter into the flour with your fingertips until you get a breadcrumb consistency. Gradually stir in up to 125ml/4fl oz/½ cup of water, mixing it in with your hands until you get a smooth dough that isn't sticky. Cover and chill in the fridge for 20 minutes to relax the pastry (grab a cuppa and relax yourself, too).

3   Preheat the oven to 190°C/170°C fan/gas 5 and line a large, flat baking sheet with baking paper.

4   Dust your work surface with flour and roll out your pastry so it's around 3mm/⅛ in thick. Cut out circles by cutting around an 18cm/7in plate or cake tin base. Re-roll the pastry and continue to cut circles until it's all used up – you need four circles. Put around 3 tablespoons of the filling onto one half of each pastry circle leaving a 2cm/¾in border, brush the beaten egg around the border and then fold the other half of the pastry circle over the top of the filling. Either crimp the edges or press them together with a fork.

5   Place the pasties onto the lined baking sheet about 4cm/1½in apart. Brush all over the tops with the egg wash, then poke a couple of holes in the top of each one to let the steam out. Bake for 35–40 minutes until the pastry is golden. Leave to cool slightly, then serve. Store cold leftovers in an airtight container in the fridge for up to 3 days.

TIP You can freeze these pasties after the egg wash point (middle of step 5), wrapping tightly so they don't get freezer burn. Bake from frozen at 200°C/180°C fan/gas 6 for 40–45 minutes until golden and cooked through.

GF DF

A light and fluffy, rich chocolate cake that has a delicious mousse-like texture and is not overly sweet, this is the stuff dreams are made of. It also happens to be dairy and gluten free!

FLOURLESS HAZELNUT CHOCOLATE CAKE

SERVES 8–10
PREP 25 mins, plus cooling
COOK 45 mins

2 tbsp unsweetened cocoa powder, plus extra for dusting
125g/4½oz/⅔ cup, plus 2 tbsp caster sugar
250g/9oz dark chocolate, roughly chopped (dairy free if needed)
100ml/3½fl oz/generous ⅓ cup olive oil, plus extra for greasing
100ml/3½fl oz/generous ⅓ cup strong brewed coffee, cooled
1 tsp vanilla paste
1 tsp fine sea salt
6 large eggs, separated
80g/3oz/¾ cup ground toasted hazelnuts (see Tip)

1 Preheat the oven to 180°C/160°C fan/gas 4. Mix the cocoa powder with the 2 tablespoons of caster sugar. Grease a 23cm/9in loose-based round cake tin with oil and line the base with a circle of baking paper, then brush more oil on top. Tip the cocoa powder/sugar mixture into the tin and rotate the tin around so you have a thin coating all over. This will help it to rise.

2 Put the chocolate, olive oil, coffee, vanilla and salt into a large, heatproof bowl and place over a saucepan containing a little water (making sure the water isn't touching the bowl). Put over a low heat and gently melt everything together. Set aside to cool slightly.

3 Put the egg whites into the bowl of a stand mixer (or use a large bowl and an electric whisk). Whisk on a slow speed for around 2 minutes until the egg whites turn foamy. Turn the speed up to medium and slowly add the remaining 125g/4½oz/⅔ cup of sugar, 1 tablespoon at a time, until you have a smooth, thick, glossy meringue – don't over-whisk, otherwise it'll be difficult to incorporate.

4 Whisk the egg yolks into the cooled chocolate mixture, then stir in the ground hazelnuts until combined. Stir in a third of the meringue mix to loosen the chocolate batter. Tip in the rest of the meringue and fold in using a spatula until you have a light chocolatey batter. Tip into your prepared tin and spread it evenly.

5 Bake for 40–45 minutes until risen and a skewer inserted into the centre comes out clean. Run a small, sharp knife around the edge of the cake when it's hot as this will help it to sink evenly – the sponge will sink and crack significantly as it cools. Leave to cool completely in the tin, then turn out, dust with cocoa powder and slice to serve. Store in an airtight container (or wrapped) for up to 4 days.

TIP If you can't find any ground toasted hazelnuts, buy some blanched hazelnuts, toast them in a hot frying pan and leave to cool, then blitz them to a powder in a food processor.

COMFORT FOOD

A crumble cake was something that was always sold in the first little bakery I worked at when I was about 16. I've taken the basic crumble cake to the next level by adding some bonus ingredients – the crème fraîche adds a richness to the sponge and the cornflour helps create a light, fluffy texture. These, combined with the sharp fruity blackberries and crisp crumble topping, make it the dream cake.

FLUFFY BLACKBERRY CRUMBLE CAKE

SERVES 9
PREP 25 mins, plus cooling
COOK 1 hour

For the sponge

100g/3½oz crème fraîche, plus (optional) extra to serve
grated zest of 2 oranges
150g/5½oz/⅔ cup unsalted butter, softened, plus extra for greasing
150g/5½oz/¾ cup caster sugar
2 tsp vanilla paste
2 eggs
150g/5½oz/generous 1 cup self-raising flour
2 tbsp cornflour
½ tsp baking powder
a pinch of fine sea salt
200g/7oz fresh or frozen (defrosted) blackberries

For the crumble

100g/3½oz/¾ cup plain flour
50g/1¾oz/¼ cup caster sugar
60g/2¼oz/¼ cup unsalted butter, cold and cubed
a pinch of fine sea salt
2 tbsp demerara sugar (optional)

1 Preheat the oven to 180°C/160°C fan/gas 4 and grease a 20cm/8in loose-based square cake tin with butter and line with baking paper. For the sponge, put the crème fraîche into a bowl, stir in the orange zest (zest the oranges straight into the bowl, if you like) and set aside.

2 Add the butter, sugar and vanilla into a mixing bowl and beat with an electric mixer (or a wooden spoon and some muscle) for 5 minutes until pale and fluffy, making sure you scrape down your bowl to combine everything. Gradually beat in the eggs, one at a time, until smooth. Tip in the flour, cornflour, baking powder and salt and fold into the mixture. Fold in your orangey crème fraîche.

3 Tip into the prepared cake tin and level with the back of a spoon. Evenly scatter the blackberries on top.

4 To make the crumble topping, put the flour, caster sugar, butter and salt into a bowl and rub together with your fingertips until you get a crumble mixture, then keep going, pushing the crumbs together until it starts to develop into bigger pieces of crumble. Evenly sprinkle the crumble on top of the blackberries and sponge mixture, then sprinkle over the demerara sugar, if you have any.

5 Bake for 1 hour until golden brown and a skewer inserted into the centre comes out clean. Leave to cool completely in the tin, then remove and cut into 9 squares. Serve with some crème fraîche, if you like. Keep in an airtight container for up to 4 days.

TIP The amazing baker, Holly Cochrane, taught me to add your zest into the dairy. I add it into the crème fraîche here, as the fat lipids preserve and intensify the flavour, locking in the orange flavour when it bakes.

Not much beats a classic carrot cake, so I wanted to make a perfect one that was simple to make, moist, light and fluffy and didn't have any of the extra bits, like sultanas and walnuts. My friend Laura's mum said 'How can it be so light and moist? This is seriously the best cake I've eaten in a long time' – so trust the words of Mamma Tracy.

EASY CARROT CAKE

SERVES 8
PREP 25 mins, plus cooling
COOK 1 hour 10 mins

For the sponge

100g/3½oz/scant ½ cup
    full-fat Greek yogurt
grated zest of 2 oranges
150ml/5fl oz/⅔ cup vegetable
    oil, plus extra for greasing
2 eggs
100g/3½oz/½ cup caster
    sugar
100g/3½oz/½ cup soft light
    brown sugar
200g/7oz carrots, tops cut off
    and coarsely grated
225g/8oz/1¾ cups self-raising
    flour
1 tsp baking powder
2 tsp ground cinnamon

For the icing

75g/2¾oz/⅓ cup unsalted
    butter, softened
75g/2¾oz/generous ½ cup
    icing sugar
1 tsp vanilla paste or extract
150g/5½oz/⅔ cup full-fat
    cream cheese

1   Preheat the oven to 180°C/160°C fan/gas 4. Grease a 900g/2lb loaf tin (about 29 x 15.5 x 7.5cm/11½ x 6 x 3in) with oil and line with baking paper (or use a loaf tin liner). For the sponge, mix together the yogurt and orange zest in a large bowl, then set aside for 5 minutes.

2   Whisk the oil, eggs and caster sugar into the orangey yogurt. Crumble in the brown sugar so it's not lumpy and whisk into the mix. Fold in the carrots, flour, baking powder and cinnamon. Tip into the lined tin and spread evenly, then bake for 1 hour 10 minutes until it's golden and a skewer inserted into the centre comes out clean.

3   Cool in the tin for 10 minutes, then turn out onto a wire rack and leave to cool completely.

4   To make the icing, beat together the butter, icing sugar and vanilla in a bowl with an electric whisk (or a wooden spoon and some muscle) for around 4 minutes until pale and fluffy. Beat the cream cheese in a separate bowl to loosen, then add into the butter mix and whisk for 4 minutes until it's pale, thick and fluffy.

5   Spread the icing evenly on top of the carrot cake, then slice to serve. Keep in an airtight container in the fridge for up to 4 days.

TIP Combining the orange with the yogurt at the beginning helps the flavour to intensify.

I truly believe there's nothing easier than a crumble and I wanted to write one universal recipe that can use up any fruit you have left over or going spare (aside from maybe bananas and citrus, as that would be rogue). The cornflour is a great trick as it helps thicken the juices that get released. Delicious served with my Old-school Custard on page 132.

FRIDGE RAID CRUMBLE

SERVES 6–8
PREP 15 mins
COOK 45 mins

For the filling

500g/1lb 2oz fresh or frozen fruit (anything mix you have left over; if it's something like an apple or stone fruit, peel [for apples], core/stone and dice into 1cm/½in chunks)

grated zest and juice of 1 lemon

2 tbsp cornflour

50g/1¾oz/¼ cup caster, soft (light or dark) brown or granulated sugar

For the topping

150g/5½oz/generous 1 cup plain flour

75g/2¾oz/⅓ cup caster, soft (light or dark) brown or granulated sugar

¼ tsp fine sea salt

100g/3½oz/scant ½ cup unsalted butter, cold and cubed

2 tbsp demerara sugar (optional)

1 Preheat the oven to 190°C/170°C fan/gas 5. For the filling, prepare the fruit, if required. You don't have to defrost the fruit if it's frozen, unless it's frozen whole (larger fruit like plums, etc). Toss the fruit with the lemon zest and juice, cornflour and sugar, then tip into a medium baking/casserole dish (mine is around 25 x 18 x 6cm/10 x 7 x 2½in).

2 To make the topping, mix the flour, sugar and salt in a bowl. Add the butter and rub in with your fingertips until you get a crumble mixture, then keep going, pushing the crumbs together until it starts to develop into bigger pieces of crumble.

3 Sprinkle the crumble evenly over the fruit, then top with a sprinkling of demerara sugar, if you have any. Bake for 35–45 minutes until the crumble is golden and the fruit underneath is soft. This is best served warm, but it can also be enjoyed cold. Store in an airtight container (or covered) in the fridge for up to 4 days. Reheat (if desired) until hot through.

Memories flash back to school, queuing up for a warm slice of cake doused in a very thick, luminous yellow custard. This really was the beginning of my food journey – if you could call it that. It's that thick, yellow vanilla custard that now provides ultimate comfort. I've made kilos of the fancy French crème anglaise custard, but it NEVER really hits the spot the way the school custard did, because what's really missing from the posh custard is the thick starchy element.

OLD-SCHOOL CUSTARD

MAKES around 400ml/
  14fl oz/scant 1¾ cups
PREP 2 mins
COOK 5 mins

150ml/5fl oz/⅔ cup full-fat
  milk
150ml/5fl oz/⅔ cup double
  cream
1 tsp vanilla paste
3 large egg yolks
50g/1¾oz/¼ cup caster sugar
1½ tsp cornflour

1 Put the milk, cream and vanilla into a saucepan and bring to the boil over a medium heat, stirring occasionally so it doesn't stick, then turn down to a simmer.

2 While you're waiting for it to simmer, put your egg yolks and sugar into a medium, heatproof bowl and whisk for a few minutes until they start to turn pale and thick, then whisk in your cornflour.

3 Pour a quarter of the hot milk over the egg mixture and whisk so everything combines. Turn the heat down to low, then gradually pour the egg mixture back into the pan, whisking all the time.

4 Continue to whisk/stir for around 2 minutes until the custard thickens. Remove from the heat and pour the custard over your dessert. You can cool and keep this covered (with a piece of baking paper placed on the surface to stop a skin forming) in the fridge for up to 3 days, then reheat in a saucepan over a low heat until hot.

A thick, creamy, rich, salted chocolate custard is the perfect thing to pour over puddings, or if you're like me, drink from a mug.

SILKY CHOCOLATE CUSTARD

MAKES around 500ml/
18fl oz/generous 2 cups
PREP 2 mins
COOK 10 mins

200ml/7fl oz/generous ¾ cup
full-fat milk
200ml/7fl oz/generous ¾ cup
double cream
1 tsp vanilla paste
3 large egg yolks
50g/1¾oz/¼ cup caster sugar
2 tsp unsweetened cocoa
powder
50g/1¾oz dark chocolate,
finely chopped
¼ tsp fine sea salt

1 Put the milk, cream and vanilla into a saucepan over a medium heat and bring to a simmer, stirring occasionally so it doesn't stick.

2 Meanwhile, put your egg yolks, sugar and cocoa powder into a medium, heatproof bowl and whisk for a few minutes until they start to turn pale and thick.

3 Pour half of your hot milk over the egg mixture and whisk so everything combines. Turn the heat down to low and, while whisking, gradually pour the egg mixture into the pan of milk.

4 Continue to stir for around 3–4 minutes until the custard thickens. Add in your dark chocolate and salt and whisk until melted and you have a thick, creamy, dark chocolate custard. Pass through a fine mesh sieve and serve warm. You can keep this covered (with a piece of baking paper over the top to stop a skin forming) in the fridge for up to 3 days, then simply reheat gently in a saucepan to serve.

This is a cake you probably had at school, but I've taken it to the next level to make it fluffy and light but still keeping the nostalgic icing and sprinkles. I find it best served slathered in thick custard (see my Old-school Custard on page 132) or my rich, creamy Silky Chocolate Custard (page 133) for the true retro canteen experience.

SCHOOL CAKE

SERVES 15
PREP 25 mins, plus cooling and setting
COOK 30 mins

150ml/5fl oz/⅔ cup milk
juice of ½ lemon
3 eggs
1 tbsp vanilla paste
75ml/2½fl oz/5 tbsp vegetable or rapeseed oil
75g/2¾oz/⅓ cup unsalted butter, melted and cooled slightly, plus extra for greasing
225g/8oz/generous 1 cup caster sugar
225g/8oz/1¾ cups self-raising flour
1 tsp baking powder
200g/7oz/scant 1½ cups icing sugar, sifted
sprinkles, to decorate

1   Preheat the oven to 180°C/160°C fan/gas 4. Grease a 30 x 20 x 5cm/ 12 x 8 x 2in rectangular cake tin with butter and line with baking paper. Put the milk and lemon juice into a large mixing bowl and leave to sit for 1 minute to curdle slightly. Whisk in the eggs, vanilla, oil and melted butter until combined. Tip in the sugar, flour and baking powder and whisk in until there are no lumps of flour.

2   Tip the batter into the prepared tin and level with the back of a spoon. Bake for 25–30 minutes until golden and a skewer inserted into the centre comes out clean. Leave to cool completely in the tin, then turn out onto a serving plate or board.

3   Mix the icing sugar with 2–3 tablespoons of water until you get a thick icing. Spread it over the top of the cooled cake, leaving a little gap at the edge in case it runs slightly. Cover the icing with sprinkles, leave for an hour to set (if you can wait) and then cut and enjoy, with custard, if you like. Store in an airtight container for up to 3 days.

DF

Yes, I know this is technically a Swiss roll served warm with custard, but I never have suet in the cupboard, so I thought I'd avoid using it all together. The result is this lighter jam roly-poly, which achieves the nostalgic feel of a school jam roly-poly, without being too stodgy and having to steam it for HOURS. And technically it is a jam roly-poly… it has jam, and it's rolled.

LIGHTER JAM ROLY-POLY

SERVES 8
PREP 25 mins, plus cooling
COOK 11 mins

3 large eggs
120g/4¼oz/scant ⅔ cup caster sugar, plus extra for sprinkling
30ml/1fl oz/2 tbsp olive oil, plus extra for greasing
1 tsp vanilla paste
115g/4oz/generous ¾ cup plain flour
¼ tsp fine sea salt
200g/7oz/⅔ cup strawberry or raspberry jam, beaten to loosen

1 Preheat the oven to 190°C/170°C fan/gas 5. Grease a 33 x 23cm/13 x 9in Swiss roll tin with some olive oil and line the base with a rectangle of baking paper.

2 Separate the eggs into two large bowls, whites in one, yolks in the other. Whisk the egg whites with an electric whisk until they start to become frothy, then gradually whisk in half the caster sugar, 1 tablespoon at a time, until you have a thick, glossy meringue.

3 Using the same electric whisk (no need to wash it), whisk the yolks with the remaining sugar, the oil, vanilla and 2 tablespoons of water on a high speed for around 4 minutes until you have a thick, pale mixture. Fold in half the flour and the salt until you have no lumps and then fold in the remaining flour.

4 Beat a quarter of the meringue into the yolk mix to loosen it, then in two parts, gently fold the remaining meringue into the batter until combined and there are no streaks of meringue. Pour into your prepared tin and spread level with a spatula. Bake for 10–11 minutes until the sponge is starting to turn golden and is springy. Meanwhile, sprinkle some caster sugar onto a sheet of baking paper big enough to fit the sponge on.

5 Run a small knife around the edges to loosen the baked sponge from the tin, then tip it onto the sheet of sugared baking paper and remove the lining paper. Move the cake so the shorter side is facing you and score lightly across one of the shorter sides, continuing every 3cm/1¼in (but don't cut through) as this will prevent it from cracking when you roll it up. Spread over your jam, leaving a 1cm/½in border at the edge, then roll up from a short edge, using the baking paper to help you. Place, seam-side down, on a serving plate. Slice and serve warm with some custard (see my Old-school Custard recipe on page 132), if you like. Store any cold leftovers in an airtight container for up to 2 days.

My friend Laura has been known to have minimal things in her kitchen, as she's constantly moving flats. When she asked me what she could bake with her very few kitchen utensils, very little in her cupboards and a strange surplus of miniature jams, old-school jammy dodgers were the only option. If you're like Laura and are keen to bake something nostalgic, try out these beauties.

JAMMY DODGERS

MAKES 14–15
PREP 30 mins, plus cooling
COOK 14 mins

125g/4½oz/generous ½ cup
    unsalted butter, softened
125g/4½oz/⅔ cup caster sugar
250g/9oz/scant 2 cups plain
    flour, plus extra for dusting
2 tbsp milk
100g/3½oz/⅓ cup jam (any
    you have leftover)

1. Preheat the oven to 180°C/160°C fan/gas 4 and line two large, flat baking sheets with baking paper. Add the butter and sugar to a bowl and beat together until smooth and creamy (you can do this with a wooden spoon or an electric whisk if you have one). Add in the flour and milk and mix until you have a smooth dough.

2. To make it easier to roll out, take two sheets of baking paper and put the dough in between them. Roll out the dough so it is around 3mm/⅛ in thick. Remove the top piece of baking paper, then cut out about 28–30 rounds using a 6cm/2½in round cookie cutter (see Tip), re-rolling any off-cuts if you need to. Place half of them onto one lined baking sheet.

3. With the remaining rounds, cut out the middle of each using a 2.5cm/1in round or heart-shaped cookie cutter (you can then re-roll the dough from the middles if you like). Place these rounds onto the other lined baking sheet. Bake both sheets for 12–14 minutes until golden brown. The biscuits with the cut-out middles may need slightly less time than the whole ones.

4. Transfer to a wire rack and leave to cool. Once cool, spread about 1 teaspoon of jam onto each whole biscuit (flat-side facing up), then top each with a cut-out biscuit (flat-side facing down) so the jam peeps through the hole. Serve. Store in an airtight container for up to 4 days.

TIP If you don't have a cookie cutter to hand, you can use a glass that's about the right size, then for the smaller one, you can use the end of a plain piping nozzle or cut the middles out by hand.

COMFORT FOOD

DF V

Canned peaches scream nostalgia to me, as they used to be a treat when I was growing up and were always served with cheap supermarket own-brand ice cream. They're soft, sweet and bursting with tangy flavour, so when paired with fresh lemon, they make these muffins taste like summer. This recipe is ideal to whip up when you don't have much in, as it uses mainly storecupboard ingredients.

PEACH & LEMON MUFFINS

MAKES 12
PREP 10 mins, plus cooling
COOK 32 mins

350g/12oz/2⅔ cups self-
  raising flour
a pinch of fine sea salt
200g/7oz/1 cup caster sugar
½ tsp bicarbonate of soda
grated zest of 2 lemons
150ml/5fl oz/⅔ cup vegetable,
  olive or rapeseed oil
250ml/9fl oz/generous 1 cup
  milk (or use oat milk, if
  vegan or dairy free)
1 x 415g/14½oz can peach
  slices in fruit juice
  (250g/9oz drained weight),
  drained and roughly
  chopped

1 Preheat the oven to 180°C/160°C fan/gas 4 and put muffin cases into a 12-hole muffin tin. Put the flour, salt, sugar, bicarb and lemon zest into a large bowl and mix together. Tip in the oil and milk and fold everything together until just combined (don't overmix the batter, otherwise you may end up with heavy muffins).

2 Fold in 200g/7oz of the peaches so they're evenly distributed. Fill each muffin case three-quarters full, then put around 2 peach pieces on top of each muffin, using up the rest of the peaches.

3 Bake for 28–32 minutes until a skewer inserted into the centre comes out clean. Leave to cool completely in the tin, then remove and dig in. These are best eaten on the day they are made, but any leftovers will keep in an airtight container for up to 3 days.

One of my favourite family memories is going down to the freezing English seaside on holiday. The highlight of those trips was visiting the stall that sold fresh warm ring doughnuts coated in sugar. Pure nostalgia.

Hear me out, as I think this may be the best tip you will ever hear. You can wrap and freeze these doughnuts once they've been deep-fried and cooled before you add the sugar coating. Defrost, then pop one in a microwave oven on medium for 10 seconds, toss it in sugar and you have a light, fluffy, warm sugary doughnut for the ultimate snack. I tested this recipe A LOT of times, and consequently ate A LOT of doughnuts and I think they're just as good defrosted – doughnuts on demand forever more.

SEASIDE RING DOUGHNUTS

MAKES 12–14
PREP 35 mins, plus 1½ hours proving
COOK 15 mins (in batches)

500g/1lb 2oz/3½ cups strong white bread flour, plus extra for dusting
100g/3½oz/½ cup caster sugar
1 x 7g/⅛oz sachet easy-blend dried yeast
1 tsp fine sea salt
40g/1½oz/3 tbsp unsalted butter, cold and cubed
1 egg (60g/2¼oz – if your egg isn't quite 60g/2¼oz, make it up with milk), beaten
230ml/8¼fl oz/scant 1 cup milk, slightly warmed
1–1.5 litres/1¾–2¾ pints/generous 4 cups–generous 6 cups vegetable or rapeseed oil, for deep-frying

1   Mix the flour and 25g/1oz/2 tbsp of the sugar in a large bowl. Put the yeast on one side of the bowl and the salt on the other, mix each into the flour/sugar and then mix it all together (this stops the salt from killing the yeast). Rub in the butter with your fingertips until you have a sandy consistency.

2   Pour the egg into the mix and then gradually add in the warm milk, mixing with your hands until you have a soft dough that isn't too sticky. Tip out onto the work surface and knead for 8–10 minutes until you have a smooth dough (don't worry if it becomes stickier when the butter softens). Bring together into a ball and put back into the bowl, cover and leave to prove in a warm place for about 1 hour until almost doubled in size.

3   Cut square pieces of baking paper big enough to put each doughnut on – to keep their shape when transporting to the hot oil. Dust your work surface with flour and roll out the dough to 1cm/½in thickness. Cut out your doughnuts using an 8cm/3¼in round cookie cutter, then stamp out the centre of each round using a 3cm/1¼in round cookie cutter. Re-roll the dough until it's all used up – you should have around 12–14 doughnuts. Place each one on its own piece of baking paper. Cover and leave to prove for 30 minutes.

4   Pour the oil into a large, heavy-based saucepan, filling it half-full. Heat to 170°C (or until a piece of dough dropped into the oil bubbles immediately and turns golden within about 30 seconds). Line a tray with kitchen paper and fill a shallow bowl with the remaining sugar.

5   Put the doughnuts into the hot oil in around three batches so they don't touch. Deep-fry for 2 minutes on each side until golden, then, using a slotted spoon or spider strainer, transfer to the kitchen paper to drain off any excess oil. Ensure the oil is heated back up to temperature before frying the next batch. Toss the doughnuts in the sugar to coat and eat warm. Cool and keep any leftovers in an airtight container for up to 2 days.

TIP If you don't have any cookie cutters, divide the dough into 12 equal portions and shape each into a ball. Push one index finger through the middle of each ball to make a hole, then put your other index finger in the hole and swirl both around each other to make a 3cm/1¼in hole. Place the doughnuts on two baking trays lined with baking paper, cover and leave to prove for an hour until the dough springs back when lightly pressed. Continue as above.

A lamington is traditionally from Australia and is composed of a fluffy sponge, individually coated in chocolate and tossed in desiccated coconut, occasionally filled with jam and cream. So, I decided to create this lamington loaf instead so you only have to coat one cake, and I think it's just as delicious.

LAMINGTON LOAF

SERVES 8 generously
PREP 35 mins, plus cooling and (optional) overnight chilling
COOK 55 mins

For the sponge

200g/7oz/generous ¾ cup unsalted butter, very soft, or margarine, plus extra for greasing
200g/7oz/1 cup caster sugar
200g/7oz/1½ cups self-raising flour
3 eggs
3 tbsp milk
1 tsp baking powder
1 tsp vanilla paste

For the coating

40g/1½oz/3 tbsp unsalted butter or margarine, melted
75ml/2½fl oz/⅓ cup milk
30g/1oz/¼ cup unsweetened cocoa powder
100g/3½oz/scant ¾ cup icing sugar
100g/3½oz/1⅓ cups desiccated coconut

For the filling

300ml/10fl oz/1¼ cups double cream
1 tbsp icing sugar
150g/5½oz/½ cup jam (I like to use raspberry)

1 Preheat the oven to 180°C/160°C fan/gas 4. Grease and line a 900g/2lb loaf tin (about 29 x 15.5 x 7.5cm/11½ x 6 x 3in) with butter and baking paper (or use a loaf tin liner). Put all the ingredients for the sponge into a large bowl and beat together until you have a smooth batter (you can use a wooden spoon or an electric whisk if you have one). Tip the mix into the lined tin and spread evenly with the back of a spoon. Bake for 50–55 minutes until golden brown and a skewer inserted into the centre comes out clean. Cool in the tin for 10 minutes, then turn out onto a wire rack and leave to cool completely.

2 Make the coating. Add the melted butter or margarine, milk and cocoa powder to a wide, shallow bowl and whisk until there are no lumps. Whisk in the icing sugar until you have a smooth, thick mixture.

3 Sprinkle the desiccated coconut over a large tray. The next bit may get a little messy. Spread the chocolate mixture on all sides of the sponge cake (apart from the base) to coat, using a palette knife if you like. Leave it to set for about 15 minutes until it becomes tacky and less wet. Next, dip the cake into the desiccated coconut to coat all over, then put it back on the wire rack.

4 To make the filling, whip the cream with the icing sugar in a bowl until you have soft peaks and it just holds its shape.

5 Cut the coconut-coated sponge in half horizontally through the middle. Spread the jam over the cut-side of the bottom sponge half and top with the whipped cream, then sandwich the other sponge half on top (cut-side down). It slices a lot better once it's been in the fridge overnight, but I understand if you can't wait. Slice to serve and keep in an airtight container in the fridge for up to 3 days.

Inspired by the presentation of the tiramisu at Faros in London, where they serve the coffee-soaked savoiardi biscuits on a plate with the mascarpone cream spooned over the top, this makes tiramisu so much quicker and easier to assemble, but it's just as creamy. It's the perfect thing to serve when you need just two portions of this delicious dessert.

SPEEDY TIRAMISU FOR TWO

SERVES 2
PREP 15 mins
NO COOK

2 egg yolks
4 tbsp caster sugar
1 tbsp boiling water
75g/2¾oz/⅓ cup mascarpone cheese
4 tbsp Marsala or coffee liqueur
75ml/2½fl oz/5 tbsp double cream
4 tbsp strong brewed coffee, warm
8 savoiardi or sponge fingers
1 tsp unsweetened cocoa powder

1 Place the egg yolks and sugar into a bowl and whisk with an electric whisk for 2–3 minutes until pale and thick, adding in the boiling water halfway through.

2 Beat the mascarpone with 2 tablespoons of the Marsala or coffee liqueur to loosen, then add into the yolk mixture along with the double cream. Whisk for 1½–2 minutes until thickened but still almost pourable (at this stage, you can cover and store this in the fridge for up to a day until needed).

3 Put the coffee and remaining Marsala or coffee liqueur into a bowl and mix to combine. Dunk the sponge fingers into it for 5 seconds on each side and then place 4 onto each serving plate.

4 Spoon the mascarpone cream over the top of the sponge fingers and dust with a little cocoa powder to serve.

Sticky toffee pudding is the ultimate comforting dessert and a favourite with many people. This is my traybake version, which I make when I need a hug. A trick I learnt from the pastry team at the House of Commons was to pour some of the sticky toffee sauce on top of the sponge during the cooking process, as it goes even more caramelized and adds an extra level of moisture.

STICKY TOFFEE PUDDING TRAYBAKE

SERVES 10–12
PREP 30 mins, plus soaking
COOK 55 mins

For the sponge

400ml/14fl oz/scant 1¾ cups boiling water
250g/9oz pitted dates, roughly chopped
2 tsp bicarbonate of soda
2 tbsp golden syrup
100g/3½oz/scant ½ cup butter, softened, plus extra for greasing
125g/4½oz/⅔ cup soft dark brown sugar
125g/4½oz/⅔ cup caster sugar
3 eggs
250g/9oz/scant 2 cups self-raising flour
a pinch of fine sea salt

For the sauce

300ml/10fl oz/1¼ cups double cream
125g/4½oz/generous ½ cup unsalted butter, cubed
125g/4½oz/⅔ cup soft dark brown sugar
2 tbsp golden syrup
a pinch of fine sea salt
ice cream, custard or clotted cream, to serve

1 Preheat the oven to 180°C/160°C fan/gas 4 and grease a 30 x 20 x 5cm/12 x 8 x 2in rectangular cake tin or baking dish with butter. For the sponge, put the boiling water, dates, 1 teaspoon of the bicarb and the golden syrup into a heatproof bowl, mix and leave to sit for 20 minutes to soften and cool.

2 Put the butter and both sugars into a mixing bowl and beat with an electric whisk (or a wooden spoon and some muscle) until creamy and smooth (this will take around 8 minutes using an electric whisk). Gradually beat in the eggs, one at a time, adding 1 tablespoon of the weighed flour after each egg to avoid it splitting, until combined. Fold in the remaining bicarb, the salt and the rest of the flour until you have a smooth mixture.

3 Using a stick blender or mini chopper, blitz the date and water mixture until you get a paste. Fold this into the cake batter until combined, then tip into the lined tin and spread out so it's level. Bake for 45 minutes until almost cooked through.

4 Meanwhile, make the sauce. Put all the sauce ingredients into a saucepan and bring to the boil over a medium heat, whisking to combine. After the cake has baked for 45 minutes, pour over half of the sauce evenly and then bake the cake for another 10 minutes until a skewer inserted into the centre comes out clean and the sauce is bubbling.

5 Reheat the remaining sauce. Scoop out portions of the pudding and serve with lashings of sticky toffee sauce and some ice cream, custard or clotted cream. Store any cold leftovers in an airtight container in the fridge for up to 3 days, then reheat until hot through.

TIP Why do I add golden syrup to the sponge? Golden syrup is slightly acidic, which, when mixed with the bicarbonate of soda, creates little air bubbles and helps the sponge rise and become airy.

EASY

PUDDINGS

Sometimes after a stressful day you don't want to have to spend a long time in the kitchen but fancy something sweet after (or before, I don't judge) dinner. These desserts are perfect for that because they're easy to whip up and ideal to start with if you're a novice or slightly nervous to begin baking! From the dreamy and indulgent Mocha Self-saucing Pudding (page 156) to my quick, boozy Gin-soaked Strawberries and Cream Sundae (page 152), there's something for everyone.

CHILLED TRACKS

This super-indulgent dessert (or breakfast, if you like) has a rich, creamy chocolate custard soaked into croissants – it's the next-level bread and butter pudding you never knew you needed.

CHOCOLATE CROISSANT PUDDING

SERVES 4
PREP 5 mins, plus 30 mins soaking
COOK 40 mins

200ml/7fl oz/generous ¾ cup double cream
200ml/7fl oz/generous ¾ cup full-fat milk
150g/5½oz dark or milk chocolate, roughly chopped
1 tbsp unsweetened cocoa powder
50g/1¾oz/¼ cup caster sugar
½ tsp fine sea salt
4 croissants
4 eggs
vanilla ice cream, to serve (optional)

1 Put the cream, milk, 100g/3½oz of the chocolate, the cocoa powder, sugar and salt into a saucepan and heat over a medium heat until everything has melted together, stirring occasionally. Tip into a large, heatproof bowl and leave to cool.

2 Meanwhile, lay the whole croissants in a baking dish (mine was 25 x 20 x 4cm/10 x 8 x 1½in) and sprinkle over the remaining chocolate.

3 When the chocolate mix has cooled, whisk in the eggs and then pour this over your croissants. Cover and place a tray or dish on top, weighted down with some cans so the croissants are submerged. Leave for 30 minutes so the croissants soak up the egg mixture.

4 Preheat the oven to 180°C/160°C fan/gas 4. Bake the pudding for 20 minutes until the chocolate custard has set slightly around the edges and is glossy in the middle. Serve warm (or cold) with some ice cream, if you like. Keep any leftovers in an airtight container in the fridge for up to 3 days, then serve cold or reheat until hot through.

This is a delightfully fresh dessert! The soaked strawberries are good for eating on their own, but are taken up a notch when joined by rich clotted cream, crisp shortbread and ice cream. My favourite part is the gin syrup at the bottom of the glass, which is mixed with a little melted ice cream at the end – a little bonus treat! This recipe can easily be quartered if you want to make a quick one for yourself.

GIN-SOAKED STRAWBERRIES & CREAM SUNDAE

SERVES 4
PREP 15 mins, plus 20–40 mins or overnight soaking
NO COOK

400g/14oz fresh strawberries, hulled and halved (or quartered, if larger)
grated zest and juice of 1 lime
a handful of fresh mint, leaves picked and finely chopped
2 tbsp gin (or use elderflower cordial for an alcohol-free dessert)
2 tbsp caster sugar
4 scoops of vanilla ice cream
50g/1¾oz clotted cream
100g/3½oz shortbread, crumbled

1 Tip the strawberries, lime zest and juice, mint, gin (or cordial) and sugar into a large bowl, mix together, then leave to macerate at room temperature for 20–40 minutes until the strawberries have softened and you have a syrupy liquid, or cover and leave them in the fridge overnight.

2 Into four large glasses, layer spoonfuls of the vanilla ice cream, with little teaspoon dots of the clotted cream, a crumble of the shortbread, some of the soaked strawberries and a drizzle of the syrup. Continue layering like this until everything is used up, finishing with a spoonful of ice cream, a few strawberries and a crumble of shortbread. Serve and enjoy!

GF

This comforting and rich creamy rice pudding served with sticky honey-roasted strawberries is the ultimate pairing. You can even add a splash of milk to loosen and chill the rice pudding down for a cold summertime dessert.

HONEY-ROASTED STRAWBERRY RICE PUDDING

SERVES 4
PREP 5 mins
COOK 30 mins

For the rice pudding

550ml/19fl oz/generous 2¼ cups full-fat milk
1 tsp vanilla paste
100g/3½oz/½ cup pudding rice
100ml/3½fl oz/generous ⅓ cup double cream
2 tbsp caster sugar
25g/1oz/1¾ tbsp unsalted butter, cubed
2 tbsp shelled pistachios, toasted and roughly chopped, to serve (optional)

For the honey-roasted strawberries

400g/14oz fresh strawberries, hulled and halved
4 tbsp runny honey

1 Preheat the oven to 180°C/160°C fan/gas 4. For the pudding, put the milk and vanilla into a large saucepan over a medium heat and bring to the boil, then turn it down to a simmer. Rinse the pudding rice in a sieve until the water runs clear, then add the rice to the milk. Simmer for 20–25 minutes, stirring occasionally, until the rice is soft.

2 Meanwhile, for the strawberries, put the strawberries onto a flat baking sheet and drizzle over the honey. Roast for 25 minutes, turning over halfway through, until they are soft. Set aside until needed.

3 Stir the cream, sugar and butter into the rice pudding and simmer for 5 minutes until the butter has melted and the pudding thickens. Divide into bowls and top with the honey-roasted strawberries and a sprinkle of roasted pistachios, if you have any. Serve. Cool any leftovers and keep in an airtight container in the fridge for up to 2 days.

Whenever my household is craving something sweet and comforting, I stick one of these in the oven when I get home from work so we can devour it that evening and beyond. It's so simple to make and the gooey custardy base (made with good old custard powder) makes it nostalgic comfort food. This recipe can easily be halved.

GOOEY BANANA BREAD PUDDING

SERVES 8–10
PREP 8 mins
COOK 35 mins

For the sponge

4 ripe bananas (about 350g/12oz total unpeeled weight), mashed
275g/9¾oz/2 cups self-raising flour
1 tsp baking powder
2 tsp ground cinnamon
175g/6oz/generous ¾ cup soft light brown sugar
150g/5½oz/⅔ cup unsalted butter or margarine, melted and cooled slightly, plus extra for greasing
2 eggs, beaten

For the sauce

500ml/18fl oz/generous 2 cups boiling water
150g/5½oz/¾ cup soft light brown sugar
3 tbsp custard powder
ice cream, to serve (optional)

1   Preheat the oven to 180°C/160°C fan/gas 4 and grease a deep 2-litre/3½-pint/8½-cup casserole or baking dish (around 35 x 25cm/14 x 10in) with butter, then place it on a baking tray (this will save your oven in case the pudding bubbles over).

2   Add all the sponge ingredients into a large bowl and mix with a wooden spoon until it's all combined. Pour into the prepared tin and level with the back of a spoon.

3   Whisk all the sauce ingredients together so the custard powder dissolves, then evenly pour this over the top of the sponge mixture (it may seem strange, but it will work). Bake for 35 minutes until the sponge is golden. Serve warm (or cold) with ice cream, if you like. Cool and keep any leftovers in an airtight container in the fridge for up to 4 days. Serve cold or reheat until hot through (about 30 seconds on high in a microwave oven should do it).

While I was training to be a chef, Isla Atkins introduced me to the world of a self-saucing pudding. You don't have to faff about making a separate sauce and you can enjoy this easy pud for the ultimate comfort dessert.

MOCHA SELF-SAUCING PUDDING

SERVES 10–12
PREP 20 mins, plus resting
COOK 35 mins

For the sponge

125ml/4fl oz/½ cup milk
2 tbsp coffee granules
100g/3½oz dark chocolate, roughly chopped (optional)
30g/1oz/¼ cup unsweetened cocoa powder
225g/8oz/1¾ cups self-raising flour
1 tsp baking powder
a large pinch of sea salt flakes
125g/4½oz/⅔ cup soft light brown sugar
100g/3½oz/scant ½ cup unsalted butter, melted and cooled until tepid, plus extra for greasing
2 eggs

For the sauce

200ml/7fl oz/generous ¾ cup double cream
50g/1¾oz/3½ tbsp unsalted butter, cubed
200g/7oz/1 cup soft light brown sugar
30g/1oz/¼ cup unsweetened cocoa powder
2 tbsp coffee granules
a pinch of fine sea salt
300ml/10fl oz/1¼ cups boiling water
vanilla or coffee ice cream, to serve

1   For the sponge, heat the milk either in a microwave oven or in a saucepan until warm, stir in the coffee granules to dissolve, then leave to cool. Preheat the oven to 180°C/160°C fan/gas 4. Grease a deep 2-litre/3½-pint/8½-cup casserole or baking dish (around 35 x 30cm/14 x 12in) with butter, then place the dish on a baking tray (this will save your oven in case the pudding bubbles over).

2   Add all the ingredients for the sauce into a mixing bowl or large jug, then whisk together until the butter has melted, the sugar has dissolved and everything is combined. Set aside.

3   Now back to the sponge. Put the dark chocolate, if using, the cocoa powder, flour, baking powder, salt and brown sugar into a large bowl. You may have to crumble in the brown sugar to make sure it's not in clumps. Stir to combine.

4   Add the melted butter, the eggs and cooled coffee mixture and whisk to combine until you have a smooth batter. Tip into the prepared dish and level with the back of a spoon. Pour the sauce all over the batter (it'll seem strange, but just trust the process).

5   Bake for 30–35 minutes until the pudding is risen and the sauce is bubbling around the edges. Remove from the oven and leave to rest for 5–8 minutes to let more of the sauce soak into the sponge, then serve each portion with a scoop of ice cream. Cool and keep any leftovers in an airtight container in the fridge for up to 4 days.

TIP If you want to make this for guests, you can make the sponge mixture and sauce separately, just before everyone arrives, then midway through the main course, you can pour the sauce over and bake the pudding ready to serve for dessert.

A nostalgic classic is a squishy, soft, sweet coconut and jam pudding. But what if you could have something similar, if not better, to that comforting dessert in just a few minutes? Try this microwave pud, perfect for the times when you're craving some sweet comforting joy. A hug in a mug.

MICROWAVE SAUCY COCONUT & JAM PUDDING

SERVES 1–2
PREP 4 mins, plus cooling
COOK 1½ mins

For the sponge

1½ tbsp unsalted butter,
  melted and cooled slightly
  (you can melt the butter in
  the mug for ease)
1 tbsp caster sugar
3½ tbsp self-raising flour
a pinch of fine sea salt
1 tbsp desiccated coconut,
  plus extra to serve
2 tbsp milk

For the sauce

1 tbsp caster sugar
2½ tbsp jam (any flavour),
  beaten to loosen
a pinch of fine sea salt
2 tbsp boiling water

1 Mix all the sponge ingredients together in a large mug (around 350ml/12fl oz/1½ cups) until you get a smooth batter.

2 For the sauce, put the sugar, jam and salt into a small, heatproof bowl and pour over the boiling water, then stir until combined. Pour the sauce mix over the batter in the mug.

3 Put, uncovered, in a microwave oven and cook on high for 1½ minutes, watching to turn the microwave off before the pudding overflows, and stopping and starting the microwave in short bursts until it's just cooked through. The sponge should be just cooked on top and be sitting in a big puddle of jam sauce. Sprinkle with some extra desiccated coconut and leave the pudding to rest for around 1 minute to soak up some of the sauce before diving in.

TIP It's really important you use a tablespoon measure here and not eye it on a dessert spoon... unless you're desperate for pudding.

When you crave something hot and chocolatey but don't need to cook a pudding for the whole family, this pudding is perfect and is ready in a few minutes. The rich, gooey, fudgy warm chocolate pudding with a built-in sauce is like heaven in a mug. See also the measuring Tip opposite.

MICROWAVE SAUCY HOT CHOCOLATE FUDGE PUDDING

SERVES 1–2
PREP 4 mins, plus cooling
COOK 1½ mins

For the sponge

1½ tbsp unsalted butter, melted and cooled slightly (you can melt the butter in the mug for ease)
1 tbsp soft light brown sugar
3½ tbsp self-raising flour
a pinch of fine sea salt
½ tbsp unsweetened cocoa powder
2 tbsp milk

For the sauce

1 tbsp unsalted butter, cubed
1½ tbsp soft light brown sugar
½ tbsp unsweetened cocoa powder
a pinch of fine sea salt
40ml/1½fl oz/2¾ tbsp boiling water

1 Mix all the sponge ingredients together in a large mug (around 350ml/12fl oz/1½ cups) until you get a smooth batter.

2 For the sauce, put the butter, sugar, cocoa powder and salt into a small bowl and pour over the boiling water. Stir until it melts the butter, mixing everything together (but don't worry if the butter won't mix in fully). Pour the sauce mix over the batter in the mug.

3 Put, uncovered, in a microwave oven and cook on high for 1–1½ minutes, watching to turn the microwave off before the pudding overflows, and stopping and starting the microwave in short bursts until the sponge is fluffy but still fudgy. The sponge should be just cooked on top and be sitting in a big puddle of chocolate sauce. Leave the pudding to rest for around 1 minute to soak up some of the sauce before diving in.

Would you like to have a dessert that transports you to a happy summer holiday? Here it is! A super simple mousse that can be whipped up in no time, plus the topping can be prepared in advance, if you like, so the pineapple develops a bolder flavour. You can easily halve this recipe, too.

PINA COLADA MOUSSE

SERVES 4
PREP 15 mins, plus 30 mins or overnight soaking
NO COOK

250g/9oz fresh pineapple (prepped weight), peeled, cored and chopped into 2.5cm/1in chunks (or you can use drained, canned pineapple if you don't have fresh)
3 tbsp dark rum
grated zest and juice of 1 lime
4 tbsp soft light brown sugar
500g/1lb 2oz thick coconut cream (not milk)
1 tsp vanilla paste
4 glacé cherries, to serve (optional)

1 Put the pineapple, 2 tablespoons of the rum, the lime zest and juice and 1 tablespoon of the sugar into a bowl, stir, then leave to macerate for 30 minutes, or overnight in the fridge if you want a stronger flavour.

2 Put the remaining rum and sugar, the coconut cream and vanilla into a separate bowl and whisk together with an electric whisk for 2–3 minutes until thick and smooth. Spoon the mixture into four small shallow bowls, then top with your pineapple and a drizzle of the syrup. Finish each serving with a glacé cherry, if you like. Serve immediately.

TIP If you can't find coconut cream, take an unopened tin of coconut milk and put it in the fridge overnight. It will separate – be sure not to shake it, and you can scrape the cream off the top.

EASY PUDDINGS

Whip this up in 10 minutes and then leave it in the fridge to set until you want a snack! Sometimes you just need to use up all the sweet odds and ends lying around in your kitchen, and tiffin is perfect for that. I've been known to throw in cereal scraps, marshmallows or anything that's lying around, too (within reason).

QUICK TIFFIN

MAKES 16
PREP 10 mins, plus 3 hours or overnight chilling
COOK 5 mins

125g/4½oz/generous ½ cup unsalted butter, plus extra for greasing
½ tsp fine sea salt
50g/1¾oz/¼ cup caster, granulated or soft light brown sugar
3 tbsp golden syrup
3 tbsp unsweetened cocoa powder
225g/8oz biscuits (I normally use digestives or whatever's left in my biscuit tin)
50g/1¾oz dried fruits or nuts, roughly chopped if larger
250g/9oz dark or milk chocolate, melted
1 tsp sea salt flakes (optional)

1   Grease a 20cm/8in loose-based square cake/baking tin with butter and line with baking paper. Put the butter, fine salt, sugar, golden syrup and cocoa powder into a saucepan and cook over a medium heat, stirring occasionally, until everything has melted together.

2   Meanwhile, crush your biscuits – I usually put them in a ziplock bag and whack them with a rolling pin (great to let out some anger, too). Be sure to leave some more chunky for a bit of extra texture.

3   Once your butter mix has melted, stir in the dried fruits or nuts and crushed biscuits until everything is coated. Pour into your lined tin and use the back of a spoon to spread evenly, pressing down so it's smooth and level on top.

4   Pour the melted chocolate on top and smooth it over in an even layer using a spoon or palette knife. Sprinkle over the sea salt flakes, if using, then chill the tiffin in the fridge for 3 hours or overnight to set completely.

5   Turn out of the tin, peel off the lining paper and slice into 16 squares using a hot knife. Store in an airtight container in the fridge for up to 4 days.

TIP *If you dunk your tablespoon measure into a mug of boiling water and then use it, it'll help the golden syrup slide off the spoon more easily.*

This Portuguese dessert is the perfect thing when you're in a rush but want to create a satisfying dessert. It's moreish, yet it's so simple. Traditionally, Maria biscuits are used, but I've found rich tea biscuits to be the most similar, although you can change it up and use any biscuits you like! You can even top the Serradura with the gin-soaked strawberries from the Gin-soaked Strawberries and Cream Sundae recipe on page 152.

SERRADURA

SERVES 2–4
PREP 10 mins
NO COOK

200ml/7fl oz/generous ¾ cup
    double cream
150g/5½oz condensed milk
1 tsp vanilla paste
100g/3½oz rich tea biscuits,
    Hobnobs or digestives (or
    Maria biscuits, if you can
    find them)
fresh berries and fresh mint
    sprigs, to serve (optional)

1 Whip together the double cream, condensed milk and vanilla in a bowl using an electric whisk (or by hand if you're feeling strong) until soft peaks form and it's just starting to hold its shape.

2 Put the biscuits into a food processor and blitz until you have fine crumbs, or put into a ziplock bag and bash with a rolling pin.

3 Get 2 larger or 4 small tumblers and layer the sweetened cream mixture and the biscuit crumbs in the tumblers, so you have about 6–7 layers in each glass. You can top these desserts with anything you like, but I enjoy adding berries and mint for a bit of freshness. Eat right away or you can store leftovers (covered) in the fridge overnight and enjoy the next day.

TIP *You can use a piping bag fitted with a plain nozzle to get the cream layers into the glasses, if you'd like them to be neater.*

My grandfather is from Austria, and this was one of the breakfasts his mother used to make for him, but I now cook it as a speedy dessert, too. It's similar to a chopped-up pancake soufflé but with the addition of rum-soaked raisins (which can be optional, but I highly recommend them).

KAISERSCHMARREN

SERVES 2
PREP 15 mins, plus soaking
COOK 10 mins

50g/1¾oz/⅓ cup raisins
2 tbsp dark rum
150ml/5fl oz/⅔ cup milk
2 eggs, separated
a pinch of fine sea salt
50g/1¾oz/¼ cup, plus 1 tbsp caster sugar
150g/5½oz/generous 1 cup self-raising flour
25g/1oz/1¾ tbsp unsalted butter

To finish and serve
1 tbsp icing sugar
full-fat natural yogurt and fresh berries (optional)

1 Put the raisins and rum together in a small bowl and leave to soak until needed (this can be done a day in advance, if you like, and left at room temperature).

2 Put the milk, egg yolks, salt and the 50g/1¾oz/¼ cup of caster sugar into a mixing bowl and whisk together for 2–3 minutes until starting to turn pale. Put the egg whites into a separate bowl and whisk using an electric whisk until they are thick and holding their shape. Gently whisk the egg whites into the egg yolk mixture. Drain the raisins and add the rum soaking liquid to the egg mix. Sift in your flour and whisk carefully until combined.

3 Put a large frying pan over a low-medium heat and add in the butter until melted, then pour in all of your batter and top with the rum-soaked raisins. Fry for 4–5 minutes until it's bubbling and starting to set around the edges. Using a spatula (or two) with a confident motion, flip the pancake over and fry for a further 3 minutes. Sprinkle the remaining 1 tablespoon of caster sugar over the top.

4 The traditional way to cut up the Kaiserschmarren is to use two spatulas and drag them through the mixture in opposite directions. Or you can flip it onto a board and cut it in half down the centre and then into strips using a sharp knife. To finish, dust with the icing sugar and serve warm with yogurt and berries on the side, if you like.

Sometimes you don't want a big dessert after a heavy dinner but still fancy a sweet treat to finish the meal. These date and peanut butter chocolate bites are perfect for those meals and are full of sweet, salty goodness. This recipe is easily doubled.

5-MINUTE PEANUT BUTTER BITES

SERVES 2
PREP 5 mins, plus setting
NO COOK

6 dates, split open
    lengthways and pitted
3 tsp peanut butter
50g/1¾oz dark chocolate,
    melted (vegan or dairy free
    if needed)
1 tsp sea salt flakes

1 Slightly break open each of the dates and place ½ teaspoon of peanut butter in the middle of each one, then press the date halves together again to enclose the filling inside.

2 Lay a sheet of baking paper on a plate. Dunk the dates into the melted chocolate to coat and place on the baking paper. Sprinkle them with sea salt flakes, then put them in the fridge to set. Keep in an airtight container in the fridge for up to 4 days.

DIETARY INDEX

If you're cooking for someone with a dietary need, this index shows you the ideal recipe to suit those needs, or recipes that can be adapted easily.

GLUTEN-FREE RECIPES (GF)

VEGAN RECIPES

DAIRY-FREE RECIPES

TIN INDEX

At at-a-glance guide to equipment needed for each recipe, so you can choose the recipe that suits according to what you already have in the kitchen.

INDEX

TERMS AND TRANSLATIONS

British Ingredients
Bicarbonate of soda
Biscuits
Biscuit tin
Caster sugar
Cornflour
Coriander (fresh)
Dark chocolate
Demerara sugar
Desiccated coconut
Digestive biscuits
Double cream
Dried chilli flakes
Easy-blend dried yeast
Flaked almonds
Ginger biscuits
Golden syrup
Icing sugar
Jammy dodgers
Mixed spice
Plain flour
Self-raising flour
Spring onions
Sultanas

American Ingredients
Baking soda
Cookies
Cookie jar
Superfine sugar
Cornstarch
Cilantro
Bittersweet chocolate
Raw brown sugar
Dried unsweetened shredded coconut
Graham crackers
Heavy cream
Hot red pepper flakes
Fast-action dried yeast
Sliced almonds
Ginger thins
Light corn syrup
Confectioners' sugar
Jelly ring cookies
Apple pie spice
All-purpose flour
Self-rising flour
Scallions
Golden raisins

British Equipment
Cake tin
Clingfilm
Loaf tin
Muffin tin
Nozzle
Piping bag
Swiss roll tin
Tart tin

American Equipment
Cake pan
Plastic wrap
Loaf pan
Muffin pan
Piping tip
Pastry bag
Jelly roll pan
Tart pan

ACKNOWLEDGEMENTS

If you're reading this now, thank you for supporting me and coming on this culinary journey. I hope that this book brings you joy and gives you the confidence to bake for your friends and family to spread the love. Whether you've followed my recipes for the past decade (back when I had a food blog called Fashionable Food – no one laugh) or are new to the club – welcome! I can't wait to see what you create.

We joked that this would be my version of an Oscar's speech, but this book wouldn't have come together without the help of so many incredibly talented people – so here we go!

Holly Cochrane, you food-styling artist, multi-tasking queen and beacon of crazy career stories. Words cannot convey how grateful I am to have you on this team, your ability to bring recipes to life in such a stunning way will never fail to amaze me. I've learnt a lot from you – thank you.

The photography icon, **Lizzie Mayson**. I know I mentioned it most days on the shoot, but you are a wizard when it comes to lighting. Thank you for being a pivotal light in this project, it's been a joy to see how passionate you are about creating beautiful photos and I hope you love how it's all come together.

To the woman who loves pink just as much as I do, **Louie Waller**. Without you and your keen eye for gorgeous props this book wouldn't be as stunningly aesthetically pleasing as it is. Thank you for battling train strikes to get to the shoot and always arriving with a smile.

To photography assistants **Matthew Hague** (and hand model extraordinaire), **India Whiley-Morton** and **Elliya Cleveley**, thank you for bringing the good vibes and always being a joy to work with.

The chicest designer around, **Alice Kennedy-Owen**, I thank you for working tirelessly creating this work of art and coping effortlessly with all the twists and turns of the project. You're insanely talented.

To the remarkable editor, **Lucy Smith**, thank you for your keen eye and being a steady focused legend during the changes of the book, I've loved working with you.

Stephanie Milner and team Pavilion, thank you for your dedication to this book during our many meetings, you're a powerhouse and I'm grateful to have learnt from you.

Cara Armstrong, thank you for believing in this book way back in 2021 and for kick-starting the project, I am grateful for your honed guidance and vision.

Sophie Denmead, you worked hard assisting Holly on the shoot to make the food look gorgeous, thank you for killing it, keeping the kitchen clean and being a mop queen!

I owe a dept of gratitude to my group of devoted recipe testers who have tirelessly tested the recipes in their kitchens to make sure they work for everyone, no matter their kitchen equipment. Including **Emma Foster, Amy Page, Jade Boswell, Cybi, Corinne Abrahams, Karla Zazueta, Isabel de Bono, Amelia, Katherine Andrews, Jessica Gray, Laura Nickoll, Shadie, Chahine, Danika Briggs, Faye Hardy, Izzy Bone, Leila Lawson, Rachel Hagreen, my dear Mum, Miriam Nice, Laura Jenkins, Ella Vize, Bea Phillips, Naomi Spaven** and **Vikki West.**

My dearest Hafer Road girls, **Alice, Jen, Tracey** and **Beth**, thank you for sticking by me while I turned our old tiny London flat into a test kitchen for the book. A special thanks to the community of dedicated eaters who I can always rely on to help devour all the cakes coming out of the kitchen, sometimes five a day! **Izzy**, **Danny**, **Jess**, **Alex**, **Jodi** and **the staff at the Everyman Cinema Chelsea**, **Connor**, **Amy**, **Emily** and everyone who is part of my Southwest London food collection WhatsApp group – you're legends.

A very special thank you to my pals **Laura Jenkins**, **Ella Vize** and **Nadiya Ziafat** for being eagle-eyed copy reading icons and looking through the proof of the book – I owe you all a drink and/or a piece of cake. I'm lucky to have had a helping hand (literally) from my hand model friends **Connor Carson**, **Tracey Raye**, **Dilly Kular**, **Nadiya Ziafat** and **Silé Edwards**, thank you for your stunning work.

Back to where it all began, **Sue Yeates**, **Jacqui Holland** and **Ash Spencer** – I hope I did you proud, chefs. Sorry, there isn't a bavarois or langue de chat recipe in the book – I thought I'd leave those to the masters to teach. **Andy Ditchfield**. Chef, can you believe there's even a custard recipe in the book?! I've come a long way since lumpy custard from the House of Commons days. Thank you for everything you taught me that helped to shape the baker I am.

I'm grateful to a dream team who taught me how to write failproof recipes – **Cassie Best**, **Barney Desmazery**, **Anna Glover**, **Esther Clark**, **Adam Bush**, **Miriam Nice** and **Lulu Grimes**, while at BBC Good Food. Thank you for helping me grow in the food-writing world and being patient teachers (and for letting me play ABBA in the test kitchen).

Judi, **Zoe** and **Kane**, thanks for being my support system, from lifts to the station in the early hours of the morning to get to the kitchens, to recipe taste testing and positive support.

Mum, this book is dedicated to you – you've been my biggest cheerleader and support system all the way through from when I was training to be a chef to writing this book. Thank you for your unwavering belief in me and constant phone calls when I'm filled with doubt, I love you and owe you more than you know.

Bapa, even though you're not here to read it, I hope you're looking down, proud of the book and me. Thank you for showing me traditional Austrian recipes you grew up with, I hope I've done them justice.

Without these three people and the fate that I met them, I would've never considered writing a book:

Chris Manby, the lady who first sprinkled the idea of writing a book into my head while at dinner on a cruise press trip in 2019, after laughing about the time I was locked in a freezer. I owe you more than you know. You helped bring me confidence and knowledge about how publishing worked and were always a cheerleader.

Anna Barrett, you angel, I feel like it was fate that we met on a retreat in Madeira where I told you about wanting to write a book and you made it your mission to help find me an agent. I thank you for being encouraging and for writing Mushens on your list, where I found Silé.

Silé Edwards, what a journey! Thank you for your unwavering faith in me, for being such a powerhouse in this whole process and for suggesting writing a baking book in the first place.

ABOUT THE AUTHOR

Liberty started her career at the age of 16 when she left school to train at the prestigious Westminster Kingsway College in London for three years, studying a chef diploma that the likes of Jamie Oliver and Ainsley Harriot had previously attained. With ambitions of becoming a Michelin-Star chef, she worked in the kitchens of hotels such as The Ritz, The Jumeirah and The Conrad before settling in as a full-time pastry chef at the House of Commons in London. While she enjoyed the adrenaline of the kitchens and learnt a lot from her time working with many talented chefs, she then had the opportunity to work at BBC Good Food.

In 2018, Liberty joined the BBC Good Food Team, where she started her new food journalism career, testing every recipe that went into the magazine, and learnt how to meticulously test a recipe so it worked perfectly for the readers at home. Later, she progressed into writing recipes for the magazine and online, presenting at the BBC Good Food Show in the NEC arena in Birmingham and hosting one of their podcasts. You've probably made several of her recipes from BBC Good Food, like the highest-rated focaccia recipe, without realizing.

After over four years at BBC Good Food and *Olive* magazine, Liberty spread her wings and became freelance. Since starting as a freelance food writer and stylist, Liberty has written recipes for brands such as Asda, Tesco, Delish, Waitrose, Ocado and Crisp 'n Dry, and has even food-styled for the likes of Gordon Ramsay, *Sunday Brunch* and *The Great British Bake Off*.

From working as a professional chef to spending most of her career writing recipes for the UK's most popular food media brand, she can't wait to share tips and tricks she's learnt along the way in *I'll Bake!*

Liberty would love to see your creations, so please send pictures over to her @bakingtheliberty on Instagram.

CONVERSION CHARTS

WEIGHT

Metric	Imperial
5 g	⅛ oz
10 g	¼ oz
15 g	½ oz
25/30 g	1 oz
35 g	1¼ oz
40 g	1½ oz
50 g	1¾ oz
55 g	2 oz
60 g	2¼ oz
70 g	2½ oz
85 g	3 oz
90 g	3¼ oz
100 g	3½ oz
115 g	4 oz
125 g	4½ oz
140 g	5 oz
150 g	5½ oz
175 g	6 oz
200 g	7 oz
225 g	8 oz
250 g	9 oz
275 g	9¾ oz
280 g	10 oz
300 g	10½ oz
325 g	11½ oz

Metric	Imperial
350 g	12 oz
375 g	13 oz
400 g	14 oz
425 g	15 oz
450 g	1 lb
500 g	1 lb 2 oz
550 g	1 lb 4 oz
600 g	1 lb 5 oz
650 g	1 lb 7 oz
700 g	1 lb 9 oz
750 g	1 lb 10 oz
800 g	1 lb 12 oz
850 g	1 lb 14 oz
900 g	2 lb
950 g	2 lb 2 oz
1 kg	2 lb 4 oz
1.25 kg	2 lb 12 oz
1.3 kg	3 lb
1.5 kg	3 lb 5 oz
1.6 kg	3 lb 8 oz
1.8 kg	4 lb
2 kg	4 lb 8 oz
2.25 kg	5 lb
2.5 kg	5 lb 8 oz
2.7 kg	6 lb
3 kg	6 lb 8 oz

LIQUID VOLUME

Metric	Imperial
1.25 ml	¼ tsp
2.5 ml	½ tsp
5 ml	1 tsp
10 ml	2 tsp
15 ml	1 tbsp/3 tsp
30 ml	2 tbsp
45 ml	3 tbsp
60 ml	4 tbsp
75 ml	5 tbsp
90 ml	6 tbsp
15 ml	½ fl oz
30 ml	1 fl oz
50 ml	2 fl oz
75 ml	2½ fl oz
100 ml	3½ fl oz
125 ml	4 fl oz
150 ml	5 fl oz
175 ml	6 fl oz
200 ml	7 fl oz
225 ml	8 fl oz

Metric	Imperial
250 ml	9 fl oz
300 ml	10 fl oz
350 ml	12 fl oz
400 ml	14 fl oz
425 ml	15 fl oz
450 ml	16 fl oz
500 ml	18 fl oz
600 ml	1 pint
700 ml	1¼ pints
850 ml	1½ pints
1 litre	1¾ pints
1.2 litres	2 pints
1.3 litres	2¼ pints
1.4 litres	2½ pints
1.5 litres	2¾ pints
1.7 litres	3 pints
2 litres	3½ pints
2.5 litres	4½ pints
2.8 litres	5 pints
3 litres	5¼ pints

LIQUID MEASURES

Metric	Imperial	Spoons/Cups
5 ml		1 tsp
15 ml		1 tbsp
30 ml	1 fl oz	5 tsp/2 tbsp
60 ml	2 fl oz	¼ cup/4 tbsp
90 ml	3 fl oz	⅓ cup
125 ml	4 fl oz	½ cup
150 ml	5 fl oz	⅔ cup
175 ml	6 fl oz	¾ cup
200 ml	7 fl oz	
225 ml	8 fl oz	1 cup
275 ml	9 fl oz	
300 ml	10 fl oz	1¼ cups
325 ml	11 fl oz	
350 ml	12 fl oz	1½ cups
375 ml	13 fl oz	
400 ml	14 fl oz	1¾ cups
450 ml	15 fl oz	
475 ml	16 fl oz	2 cups
(US: 1 pint = 16 fl oz)		
500 ml	17 fl oz	
575 ml	18 fl oz	
600 ml	1 pint	2½ cups
(UK: 1 pint = 20 fl oz)		
750 ml	1¼ pints	3 cups
900 ml	1½ pints	3½ cups
1 litre	1¾ pints	4 cups
1.2 litres	2 pints	5 cups
or 1 quart		
1.5 litres	2½ pints	

DRY VOLUME SPOONS

Food	Imperial	Spoons/Cups
Biscuit crumbs	115 g/4 oz	1 cup
Breadcrumbs, dried	140 g/5 oz	1 cup
Breadcrumbs, fresh	55 g/2 oz	1 cup
Butter	25 g/1 oz	2 tbsp
	50 g/2 oz	4 tbsp
	115 g/4 oz	½ cup
	225 g/8 oz	1 cup
Cheese, cottage, cream, curd	225 g/8 oz	1 cup
Cheese, Cheddar, Parmesan, grated	115 g/4 oz	1 cup
Cocoa powder	100 g/3½ oz	1 cup
Coconut, desiccated	90 g/3½ oz	1 cup
Cornflour	140 g/5 oz	1 cup
Courgette, grated	200 g/7 oz	1 cup
Flour, plain	140 g/5 oz	1 cup
Flour, wholewheat	165 g/5¾ oz	1 cup
Mushrooms, sliced	55 g/2 oz	1 cup
Hazelnuts, peanuts	115 g/5½ oz	1 cup
Oats, rolled	85 g/3 oz	1 cup
Olives, stone in	175 g/6 oz	1 cup
Onions, chopped	150 g/5½ oz	1 cup
Peas, frozen	115 g/4 oz	1 cup
Raisins, seedless	165 g/5¾ oz	1 cup
Long-grain, uncooked rice	200 g/7 oz	1 cup
Short-grain, uncooked rice	215 g/6¾ oz	1 cup
Granulated sugar	200 g/7 oz	1 cup
Caster sugar		200 g/7 oz
Icing sugar		115 g/4 oz
Moist brown sugar	200 g/7 oz	1 cup
Demerara sugar	200 g/7 oz	1 cup
Sultanas		175 g/6 oz

Pavilion
1 London Bridge Street
London SE1 9GF

www.harpercollins.co.uk

HarperCollins*Publishers*
Macken House
39/40 Mayor Street Upper
Dublin 1
D01 C9W8
Ireland

10 9 8 7 6 5 4 3 2 1

First published in Great Britain by Pavilion
An imprint of HarperCollins*Publishers* 2023

ISBN 978-0-00-855376-0

This book is produced from independently certified FSC™
paper to ensure responsible forest management.

For more information visit:
www.harpercollins.co.uk/green

Publishing Director: Stephanie Milner
Commissioning Editor: Lucy Smith
Design Manager: Alice Kennedy-Owen
Design Assistant: Lily Wilson
Artworker: Sophie Yamamoto
Copy editor: Anne Sheasby
Proofreader: Kate Reeves-Brown
Indexer: Ruth Ellis
Photographer: Lizzie Mayson
Photography assistants: Matthew Hague,
India Whiley-Morton and Elliya Cleveley
Food styling: Holly Cochrane
Food styling assistant: Sophie Denmead
Prop styling: Louie Waller
Production controller: Grace O'Byrne

Printed and bound in RRD China
Repro by Rival Colour Ltd, London

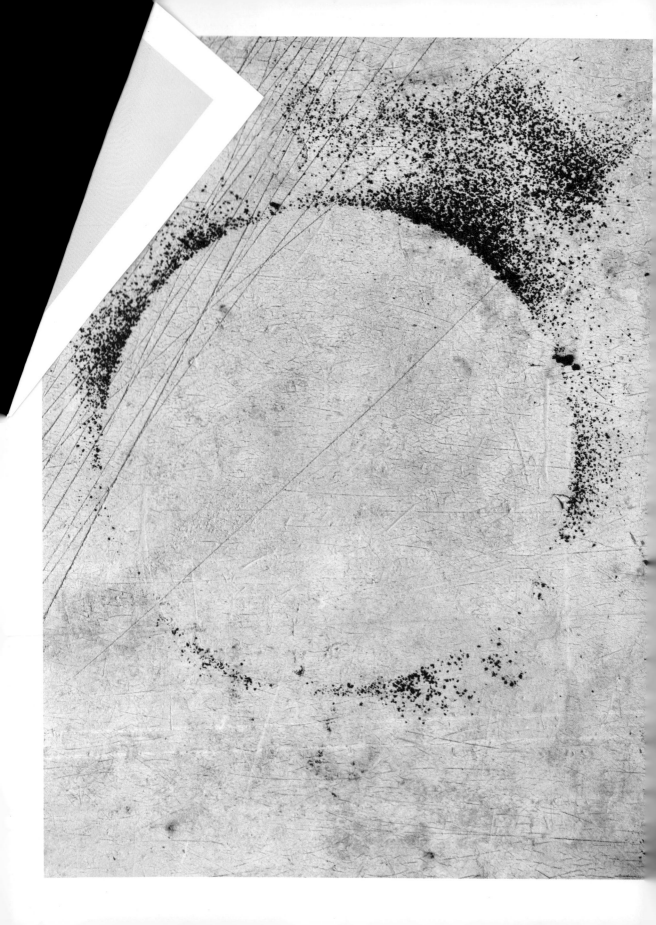